Boundaries

+

Clarity

=

Peace

Dr. Tandy Nance

About The Author

As the Founder and CEO of Life Coach Tandy, LLC, Dr. Tandy Nance is a highly accomplished and dedicated Metaphysician, Certified Holistic Life Coach, and Author. With over 18 years of experience in the mental health field, Dr. Tandy has amassed an impressive array of academic qualifications, including a Bachelor's degree in Criminal Justice, Master's degrees in Counseling Studies, Master's degree in Business Administration, and a Doctorate in Metaphysical Humanistic Science.

In addition to her extensive education, Dr. Tandy is also a Certified Emotion and Body Code Energy Healing Practitioner and a Certified Clinical Hypnotherapist. Her wealth of knowledge and expertise allows her to provide her clients with a unique and comprehensive approach to healing and personal development.

Dr. Tandy is also the author of the motivational self-help book "Boundaries + Clarity = Peace," which is designed to assist individuals who are struggling to create boundaries and gain the clarity necessary to make positive changes in their lives. Her book aims to empower people to find peace and fulfillment in their lives.

With a deep understanding of the mind, body, and spirit, Dr. Tandy's life purpose is to help others heal emotionally and move past traumatic events to fully achieve their desired life. She is passionate about empowering individuals to find their purpose and transform their lives beyond their wildest imagination. Through her unique combination of traditional and holistic techniques, Dr. Tandy is dedicated to helping her clients achieve true healing and lasting success.

Copyright Page

Dedication

This Book Is Dedicated to My Grandmother
Myrtle Corrine Hemphill and My Mother
Cheryl Ann Gaskin

Introduction

Welcome to "Boundaries + Clarity = Peace," a powerful guide to creating the life you deserve by setting clear and healthy boundaries.

Are you tired of feeling drained and exhausted by the constant demands of others? Do you feel like you're constantly giving and giving without ever getting anything in return? If so, then it's time to take control of your life and start setting boundaries that will empower you to live the life you deserve.

In this book, you'll learn the importance of creating boundaries and clarity in your life and how it leads to peace. You'll discover how to set clear and healthy boundaries with others to protect your energy and time and create a safe space for yourself.

You'll also learn how to gain clarity on what you truly want and how to achieve it. You'll discover the power of focus and how to use it to achieve your goals and create the life of your dreams.

But this book is not just about setting boundaries and gaining clarity; it's also about finding peace. When you have peace in your life, you can think clearly, make sound decisions, and take action toward achieving your goals. Peace allows you to tap into your inner strength and resilience and to find fulfillment and satisfaction in all areas of your life.

With "Boundaries + Clarity = Peace," you'll learn how to create the peaceful and fulfilling life you deserve. You'll learn how to set boundaries, gain clarity, and find peace, so that you can create the life of your dreams and live it to the fullest.

Are you ready to take control of your life and start living in peace, clarity, and purpose? Then let's begin!

Let's Begin This Journey!!!

Part One

Boundaries

"Setting boundaries is a way of caring for myself. It is self-respect and self-compassion in action."

—

Darlene Lancer

Boundary

Now I want you to sincerely Raise your hand if you ever felt like the hamster on the hamster wheel going in what seemed like a never-ending circle?

I wasn't always Coach Dr. Tandy Nance, this fine and well-put-together person. There was a time my life was in complete shambles. If you had seen me then and see me now, you would probably know that a lot of things have changed about me just because of the decision I took to better myself and fight for what is truly mine and thank goodness that I came out as a winner even though I knew that it was a tug of war. I had to compromise on many

things and simultaneously tell myself the bitter truth
I didn't want to hear or be told.

This may be precisely what you are going through
right now; I totally understand the pain you are
going through and how difficult this may be for you.
I'm here to tell you that you are not alone.

I've walked through those lonely paths thinking what
is my purpose in life? I've soaked my pillows with
intense tears from my eyes, just because I was
blinded by the things that I thought I had no control
over. I had no idea of the power that I truly
possessed. If I only knew back then the power, I had
over those things that cost me so much pain and
tears, my darkest days, would not have happened.
However, if it wasn't for my darkest moment, I
would not be the woman that I am today.

Before I go further into my story, I want you to stop
blaming yourself for everything that has happened in
your life. Take responsibility, find the tools to do
better, and move forward.

The truth is that, if you were never taught the skills,
how would you be aware of what is happening. The
next couple of sentences are going

to reveal a lot of things to you in a short while, so I want you to know that you aren't alone in this journey, and I also want you to know that you will definitely get to your destination which Is "Obtaining Peace that will come from setting boundaries and gaining clarity. So, hang on chickie, better days are coming.

I was stuck on the hamster wheel, and it was going so fast I couldn't see how to get off, and every time I thought there was an opportunity to get off, the wheel sped up even faster. Before I knew it, I was married and divorced twice, overweight, weighing over 170 pounds which may not sound like a lot, but on a 5'1 frame, and I was a single mother. This left me feeling broken, insecure, and like a failure.

You will possibly see yourself in my story or you've experienced something similar to it. All of the above happened to me during the course of years, and I didn't realize what was happening because everything was moving like a flash before my eyes.

It may feel like your life is just passing by and life is just happening to you, but don't worry, chickie, you will soon get down from that hamster wheel.

Everything is going to be just fine no matter what. you're going to take back your life, your power, your will, your space, and everything that you might have thought you lost along way; I assure you that by the time you're done reading this book, you're going to be okay, and you know what? The days of questioning and blaming yourself are over, that's wasted energy. I know because I also felt the exact same way you did about 13 years ago.

I hated myself then, the mistakes that I made were killing me inside. It took being introduced to energy healing for me to start a true healing journey. I know that it is possible for anyone to experience the level of peace I experienced when I started releasing negative energy and toxicity from my body. So, get ready for your transformation. Many things are about to change in your life.

You can agree that awareness is the first level in the process of change. For you to change, you must be aware of what you're changing from and into. If you are reading this book, I know that you are now aware of what you want to change from and not fully aware of what you're changing into. So, relax as I take you through this journey

Six years into my first marriage, my husband joined my father in our family business, which was started by my grandfather, the first black bail bondsman in

San Antonio. And what do you know, he gets my father's secretary pregnant; I'm pretty sure you can guess how that felt. when the man you love and also the father of your child gets another woman pregnant. That could be devastating.

So, after I cut up… Because y'all know I cut up, right???? We divorced, and I did what most women do; I started feeling rejected, less than others, and telling myself that there was something wrong with me. I didn't realize how vulnerable and insecure I was.

If you were ever in a similar situation, and took the necessary actions, it may have made you feel like you were wrong. But that's a lie. That's one of the lies you have told yourself, just as I did. But thank the universe that I have long left that reality, and I also want to use this moment to appeal to you to leave that reality and focus on something bigger, see the bigger picture for what it is; this is how you are going to get back to yourself.

Because I was feeling this way about myself, guess what I did. Unknowingly manifested and attracted someone into my life who was feeling the same way and worst about themselves. The universe will always give you what you ask for unconsciously or consciously; that's how the law of attraction works.

the moment you feel someway about yourself or something, you are directly or indirectly sending a message to the universe. The universe is like a delivery man; he will get you precisely what you order.

And that's why you need to be very conscious about how you feel about yourself and the things around you so that you don't attract crap and toxicity into your life. Chickies, did you know that we are living magnets? And we attract people and things in harmony with our current state of mind or well-being. Now ask yourself this simple question, how did you attract your current partner, if you have one. Also, ask yourself how I came to attract the job I am doing and how I attracted the kind of friends I have in my life. Take a minute to answer all the above questions.

You will find out that you attracted all those people and things to your life because, at one point in your life, you felt somehow about yourself, either good or bad. That feeling pulls things and people into your life that are in direct harmony with how you thought and felt then. So, you see how the law of attraction works.

It works whether you are aware of its potential or not. And that's why you need to start feeling good about yourself. To further clarify this explanation or demonstration, let me use a magnet as a case study; I know we are all familiar with a magnet even though we are not much into the science of the magnet. Still, we are all familiar with its attractive and repulsive force. Now then, the magnet feels the magnetic field of an object similar to it, it pulls that object towards itself, and that's what we all call attraction. Know, reread the statement, and see the term I use.

If the magnet "Feel The magnetic Field of an object similar to its own, it will attract it to itself." This is precisely how we behave and act as humans; all that is needed to attract certain things into our lives, like a magnet, is just a feeling and nothing more.

If you begin to feel a certain way about yourself, you will begin to pull or attract things and people that have the same feeling about themselves.

A magnet will repel objects that are not having similar vibrations to themselves. And that's why, as human beings, what we think or feel can influence our life. That's why if you don't think or feel that boundaries are needed in your life, you will never attract it; if you don't feel or see the need for clarity and peace, you will never attain clarity which will lead you to experience peace.

So, I want you to take charge of your thoughts and feelings because they are powerful. Guiding and protecting the things that go through your mind is important; you are a living magnet.

Because I was a living magnet, I want you to know that at that point in my life, I literally divorced the pot and married the frying pan! I ignored all the red flags to feel validated. 2 years into my second marriage, we moved from Texas, where my support system was, to Philadelphia, where I knew no one. I found myself 2000 miles away from home being emotionally, verbally, and financially abused.

I was living in pure misery. After year seven of this marriage, I finally told myself this was not what was expected of my life; this was not the woman I was expected to be; I come from royalty. Somehow by this time, I'd managed to earn two master's degrees, raise my son, and direct a mental health facility where I probably should've been a resident.

Now you see what feeling bad about myself led me to; this is why I tell my clients and people around me to stop feeling crappy about themselves because if they don't, you are going to attract garbage into your life. Don't worry when we get to the clarity section; you're going to read for yourself how this behavior works best. Even though sometimes terrible things happen to you, I immediately want you to start visualizing and feeling good about yourself.

Now let me tell you a little trick about the law of attraction. This law works best when we are at our lowest vibrations. Because when we are at our; lowest vibrations, our emotions and feelings tend to be intense at that time, and the universe will immediately start to attend to what we are thinking about and begin to deliver all that we start to think and feel about ourselves.

Here's an example of the previous statement:

the way you will get attended to at the hospital would be different if it was an emergency. That's how the universe treats us; when we are vibrating in low vibrations, the universe moves in haste to attend to us and give us what we are currently vibrating in. Whenever you feel your vibrations are low, I want you to do this. I want you to begin reciting positive affirmations while looking in the mirror.

 It may sound crazy, but it will bring your vibrations up and prevent you from manifesting negative crap into your life. Immediately when you start feeling that way, begin with some positive affirmations.

I want you to feel good about the affirmation; I want you to say it with a loud voice and feel the energy that comes with the affirmation that you are reciting, keep reciting it until your brain, and your body begins to feel good, at first, those affirmations are not going to make sense to you, but if you persist and keep reciting them, it will come a time when they begin to make sense to you and then, you can tell yourself, Well done.

There was a time when every day I began to envision what my life should look like, what the woman I was expected to be should look like, from the clothes I wore to the car I drove. As I said earlier that awareness is the first level of change. This phase was when I began to feel the need for change; this is where I began to use the power of visualization to create this new image, I wanted for myself. Understand that we are architects.

We can create and build the women we desire to be by using the power of visualization. You can use visualization to see the picture of a new you. So right now, I want you to begin to visualize what you want to look like, what kind of car you want to drive and what kind of peace and clarity you want to get.

Visualization is like having a direct line to your higher self, and I want you to learn to maximize this ability. This is the first step towards setting boundaries that will eventually lead to clarity and peace, so sit down with a pen and paper. I want you to write down all the beautiful things you love about yourself and all the great things you would love to experience.

Write down, the way you want this woman to smile, how you want her to talk, how you want her to be treated, how you want her to be respected, how you want her to carry herself because, as I've said earlier you must be aware of who you want to change to before the change can be effective.

So, take your time and begin to create those beautiful mental pictures. Write down things you know will make you feel good and excellent about yourself. Remember that the universe is listening to you, so you must intentionally because whatever you ask is what you are given, and nothing will change that.

So, go into the world of your visualization and create that perfect picture of the woman you want to be. If what you want to change is clear, setting boundaries won't be hard for you. The moment you don't see a clear picture of what you want, are the moments you won't be able to set boundaries for yourself. So, get to work now and don't stop until you know what you want for your life, don't accept mediocrity for yourself; visualize big things for your life because you're your only limitation.

There's no limit on visualization; how far you can see is directly tied to how far you can go; you need to see far so that you can go far. So, create that world of yours and make sure it is perfect in your eyes. If it's not perfect in your eyes, recreate it and keep recreating it until it becomes your version of perfect.

You will know precisely what you are up against when this is done. Because this is a war zone, and you need to identify the enemy, as I did in my situation, the enemy is not far from us; it is very close and to make things more complex, the enemy is our current state of being and we need to fight that current state of being and that current state of mind to let us go, we need to battle for our freedom and say no to whatever that is going to makes us feel like crap again.

So, go on and create what you want and believe you can create that new life for yourself, and don't listen to the naysayers.

When I began my visualization process, what I wanted and did not want for my life became clear because I was now aware of what was holding me back from getting the life I wanted.

I was now ready to regain my power, and this is where setting boundaries comes in. Boundaries will help you gain perspective on how to get your life back; boundaries will help you shield yourself from what you don't want. But for that boundary to work, you will have to know what you are creating the boundary against, and you also need to know what challenges you're up against.

Start thinking of your space as a kingdom and you are the Queen. This is how you will fight back to get your kingdom back. Always remember that you are the queen of your domain, the ruler of your kingdom, and the director of your affairs.

There was a point when I started preparing to buy a home, making my husband feel even more insecure. Listen chickies, there is something I really want you to get from this part of my story. When you start to set boundaries, the people who take advantage of you will be angry. Why? Because the gravy train is ending. And they will soon feel the effects. And it's a strong possibility that they will continue to look for ways to bring your energy down.

I want you to get ready for a challenge because setting boundaries is most definitely going to be challenging, and if you are not prepared, you will not win.

Back to the story. So, one night in the middle of the night, my husband decided to take my car while I was sleeping. The following day, he woke me up and told me he got stopped by the police with no driver's license. The car is impounded. We go before the judge and find out he owes over $2000 in fines.

My options are I pay what he owes, or he goes to jail. I told the judge, "Well, I guess he's going to jail today" they handcuffed him and started to take him where he clearly deserved to go. I'm like, okay, judge "where do I pick up my car?" The judge gave me a really confused look and said, "oh no, you still have to pay the $2000 to get the car back". I couldn't believe it; I was devastated. I had worked so hard to save money to buy a house. Only to end up spending every dime on getting my car back. I called the broker that was helping me with the purchase of the home, and I was hysterical.

Now you see what I'm talking about, the moment it's apparent that you are about to step into greatness, there will always be someone ready to snatch your energy because their goal is to bring you back to where you started, and that's why you need to be intentional in your moves; And by moves, I mean the direction you're guiding your life and the boundaries you're setting; you must be intentional and consistent as you begin the process of setting that boundary and be ready for people to challenge the boundaries you set, because they are going to put up a fight.

If they notice that you're not backing down, they will eventually give in or give up.

But that won't happen until you commit to the boundaries you create. Have you ever heard of change without a challenge? Absolutely not, Change comes with a significant amount of uncomfortableness and challenges. And that's ok, know that if you remain consistent in the journey, you will win at the end of the day.

Let me help somebody today; you don't have to know how it will happen. The "How" should be the least of your worries because the universe will place who and what you need in your path.

All that is expected of you is to take action and remain consistent with your efforts to take your life to the next level; everything will begin to make sense as you start to move forward. In the beginning the journey may still seem a bit foggy, and that's ok.

When you're starting something new or committing to making changes, most of the time you won't know where the road is going to lead you. Still, as you progress, everything will begin to make perfect sense to you, and that's when you start to experience a significant level of peace. No more worries about letting go of the past, because you are launching into a new phase of life.

I want you to know that when I called the broker, he said, "calm down, get your car back, and we will figure it out tomorrow." This man moved mountains for three months to get me into a house.

In the meantime, while he's working the deal for the house, I'm still with my husband moving in complete silence. I haven't said a word to him since I got my car back.

I remember that night saying to him, "can I ask you a question" and he responded, "I'm not answering any questions right now" he got in bed and turned over like It was nothing.

For the next three months, I moved in complete silence and slept on the couch in a shirt, tights, and a robe, And I kept my keys in the pocket of the rob. In a relationship, when you're crying, yelling, and arguing, it's obvious where you stand. But when you're silent a person has no clue what you're thinking or what your next move will be; that could be a dangerous space, and I wasn't sure what his breaking point would look like.

I remember the day he broke like it was yesterday. He asks me if I hate him; I break my three months of silence and say, "yes," then I think about it and say, "hate takes too much energy. I don't hate you; I don't have any respect for you". That enraged him. He gets up from the couch and starts throwing every piece of glass he can get his hands on. He turns my house upside down and leaves…. I could only think of cleaning it up before my son came home. He returns in the middle of the night. Whatever he didn't break earlier, he's breaking now.

My son was 16, and my immediate thought was to protect my son, who would try to protect his mother. I go outside, and there's an officer parked at the corner of the block.

The offer tells me she's busy and will call another officer. When they get there, he goes into overdrive. One of the officers says to me you can get an emergency protection order and tells me how to do it, or you can stay here and let him kill you. What would you do? 3 am I'm on this journey with my son to get a PFA.

I arrive at the courthouse, and there's a person at the front desk. I explain why I'm there, and he tells me to pick up the phone to talk to the judge. He says she usually doesn't honor PFAs for those reasons. I spoke to the judge.

I told her the same thing I told the person at the desk; she told me to tell him to let me down. I told him what the judge said, and he looked surprised. PFA granted……. But the journey didn't end there. I must go to my local precinct to get officers to enforce the orders at 4 am with my son by my side. When I got to the house with the officers, I attempted to open the door; he'd barracked himself inside.

The officers tell me they'll come back when I get the door open. How many of you know about fight or flight? That energy you get when your life is being threatened. Well, that came over me, and I got that door open.

He was still there, but by 5 am, he was gone. I packed up and put in storage what he didn't destroy. Now I'm at my girlfriend's house feeling confused and displaced. I can't go back to the place that I knew as home, can't stay with my girlfriend forever, and remember now I don't have the money for a down payment on the house.

And on top of that the next three weeks was a journey to make the temporary PFA permanent. In week one, the judge told me I must meet with my husband at the house later that evening for him to get some of his things.

I explained to the judge that it was my son's prom night, and he said, "are you going to the prom with him." In week two, he tells the same judge I'm not living in the house; the judge orders me to give him the keys to a place still in my name, and I'm still paying rent but don't feel safe enough to stay there.

In week three, my husband didn't show up to court; permanent order was granted. While I was at the courthouse waiting for the permanent order to be issued, I got a call from the broker telling me that the deal had been approved for my home and was going to close in an hour. The furthest thing from my mind was the house. I'd been through so much; my son and our safety were my only concern.

I never imagined that I would leave the courthouse that day and go close on a home with not one dollar to put towards the closing cost.

However, remember what I said earlier, the universe will always place who and what you need in your path when you need it.

*As a result of my life experiences, I developed a
formula for coaching.*

Boundaries + Clarity = Peace

We often struggle with creating boundaries because
we were taught that, as women, it is our
responsibility to sacrifice our needs for the sake of
others. Because of this, we sometimes lack the
courage to stand up and say no to what no longer
serves us or say I deserve better. Creating boundaries
is easily learned once you realize that you create
boundaries out of loving yourself or others.

We are also taught that certain people, such as family
or longtime friends, are entitled to our space, and we
are not taught healthy ways to deal with people that
bring stress or drama into our space. And we were
also taught that it is taboo to create boundaries with
the people in our lives with a title.

I want you to really take the time to envision your
space as a kingdom, and you are the Queen. As the
Queen, you get to determine who comes into your
space, stays in your space, and is banished from your
kingdom. You also get to determine how someone is
in your space.

Suppose someone creates disruption, brings toxic energy, or interferes with your peace. In that case, it is ok to remove them from your space. No one on earth is entitled to your peace of mind, including your family. So, you have to let go of that belief that everyone must have access to your space, that's a lie, and you were told that lie so that you won't prioritize your time over theirs.

There is a time when almost everyone has spoken negativity into someone's life, so from this day forth, you need to be intentional about the things you hear. Women who become great in life didn't listen to the nay-sayers. Even when negativity came their way, they overcame it.

They didn't only overcome; they became great in life. For example: Madam C. J. Walker encountered every obstacle imagined and overcame becoming the first black woman millionaire.

The movie Self Made, a depiction of her life, inspired me so much that I require my clients to watch the movie as homework.

As you begin setting boundaries in your life, I want you to shut your ears to the naysayers and people who don't add value to your life. As you read a moment ago, you are the queen of your domain, and you alone can grant people access to your space and time. And you alone can also revoke that access if you notice that they bring pain, toxicity, and stress into your space.

So, from now on, I want you to be in charge, I want you to feel in charge, and I want you to get committed to being in charge because setting boundaries comes from being in charge. So, get committed to being in charge of your space and kingdom because your space is also your peace.

You can't set boundaries in a space where you are not in charge. Imagine someone coming to set a boundary in your kingdom; Guess what? That person would be totally out of line. So, you see, you can't set boundaries on a space you don't own. So, I want you to own your space and get involved in committing to your kingdom.

Now that you have accepted that you own your space and you are the queen of your kingdom, it's time to get into setting boundaries for yourself.

But before we delve further into setting boundaries, you need to know a little more about the process of setting boundaries. When we are misinformed, we tend to act wrongly and that could lead to chaos." Information leads to transformation, so I urge you to pay close attention to the next couple of sections so that you will be properly informed on how to set boundaries for yourself. Without further ado, let us get started.

Myths About Boundary Setting

1. If I Set Boundaries, I'm Being Selfish

Many people may believe that setting boundaries is a form of selfishness, however, this is not the case. Selfishness is when an individual's own wants and needs take priority over the well-being of others. Establishing boundaries is actually the opposite, as it is an act of self-care and responsibility. By setting boundaries, we are recognizing that we have a responsibility to take care of ourselves in order to be able to properly care for others.

Boundaries allow us to say "no" to situations or individuals that may be harmful to ourselves or others. This way, we can effectively manage our

time, abilities, feelings, thoughts, and behaviors for
the benefit of all parties involved. In short,
boundaries are not a form of selfishness, but rather a
necessary tool for maintaining a healthy balance of
self-care and care for others.

2.   Boundaries are a Sign of Disobedience

Setting boundaries is not inherently disobedient, but
it can be if we use it as a reason to reject positive
opportunities for the wrong reasons. However, the
ability to decline certain requests or opportunities is
a healthy practice as it allows us to prioritize and
make room for truly valuable experiences by saying
"no" to lesser ones.

3.   If I Begin Setting Boundaries, I Will Be Hurt By Others

It is not uncommon for some individuals to react
negatively when we establish and uphold healthy
boundaries. However, it's important to remember
that boundaries serve as a measure of the quality of
our relationships. Those who are able to respect our
boundaries, even if they don't agree with them, truly
value and respect our autonomy and individuality.
On the other hand, those who cannot respect our
boundaries are revealing that they only value our

compliance and agreement, rather than truly caring for our autonomy.

4. If I Set Boundaries, I will Hurt Others

Boundaries are a means of self-protection, they are not meant to control, harm or attack others. They serve as a tool to safeguard ourselves while allowing others to take ownership of their own lives and actions. With appropriate boundaries, everyone is encouraged to take responsibility for themselves.

5. Boundaries Mean That I Am Angry

Emotions can be viewed as signals, and anger specifically is a warning that our personal boundaries may be at risk. If we don't address past instances of boundary violations, they can resurface when we feel our newly established boundaries are being challenged. By setting and maintaining healthy boundaries, we can confront and heal old wounds, ultimately leading to a reduction in overall anger.

Emotions serve as signals for our internal state. One such emotion is anger, which may arise when we sense a potential infringement on our personal boundaries. If left unresolved, unresolved past experiences of boundary violations can resurface and trigger feelings of anger when we believe our newly established boundaries are being challenged. By setting and enforcing healthy boundaries, we can address these past hurts and ultimately become less prone to anger.

6.   When Others Set Boundaries, It Injures Me

While it's true that unenforced boundaries can lead to hurt, it's important to recognize that hurt feelings may stem from our own perceptions and not necessarily the intentions or actions of others. Acknowledging hurt stemming from healthy boundaries can reveal areas within ourselves that require healing and may also reveal a tendency to avoid taking personal responsibility for our lives and actions.

7.   Boundaries Cause Feelings of Guilt

Establishing boundaries can be challenging when we feel obligated. People who care for us may give gifts of love, time, money, or other things, and we may feel a sense of obligation to return the favor. However, it's important to remember that a gift is something given without expectation of repayment. Instead of feeling guilty or indebted, the appropriate response is gratitude and appreciation.

How to deal with the guilt of setting boundaries will be discussed later in the book.

Dealing With Obstacles Of Setting Boundaries

The following are steps that you can take to confront the obstacles of setting boundaries.

1. Identify the obstacles

One important step in overcoming barriers to setting boundaries is to identify what those barriers are for you personally. Reflect on what is preventing you from effectively communicating and advocating for yourself. Consider the feelings and beliefs that might be influencing your ability to set boundaries.

For example, you may find that feelings of guilt or a belief that you should always put others' needs before your own are preventing you from setting boundaries. Additionally, you may find that certain myths, such as the belief that setting boundaries means being selfish or unkind, are impacting your ability to advocate for yourself.

Once you have identified your specific barriers, you can start to develop strategies to address them. This may include practicing self-compassion, learning assertive communication skills, or challenging limiting beliefs.

2. Outline what makes you think that the myth about setting boundaries is true.

In order to overcome any limiting beliefs or myths surrounding boundary setting, it can be helpful to evaluate where they come from. Reflect on your life experiences and consider how they may have influenced your view on setting boundaries. Think about any feedback or messages you may have received from others, both directly and indirectly, that may have reinforced these myths.

It may be helpful to think about any past experiences you may have had when trying to set boundaries. Have you experienced negative consequences or pushback when trying to advocate for yourself? If so, these experiences may have reinforced the belief that setting boundaries is not worth it.

Additionally, consider whether a lack of self-esteem or confidence is playing a role. Low self-esteem can make it harder to be proactive in getting your needs met and advocating for yourself. By identifying the root of your limiting beliefs, you can start to develop strategies to challenge and overcome them and set healthy boundaries for yourself.

3. Challenge your belief about the myth of setting boundaries

One way to overcome limiting beliefs or myths related to boundary setting is to actively challenge them. This means reminding yourself of the truth, rather than the myths. For example, instead of telling yourself that you don't deserve to get what you want, remind yourself that you do. This can be done by actively reframing your thoughts and speaking positively to yourself.

It can be helpful to make a list of these myth challenges and review them daily, until you truly believe them. Once you have internalized these positive affirmations, it can be useful to remind yourself of them when you are considering setting a boundary. This can help to counteract any negative self-talk or limiting beliefs that may be holding you back from advocating for yourself.

4. Stop Exaggerating

Another way to overcome barriers to setting boundaries is to stop exaggerating the potential negative consequences of doing so. This is known as "catastrophizing" and it often leads to feelings of anxiety and fear that prevent us from advocating for ourselves.

To stop catastrophizing, it can be helpful to get clear on what your fear is specifically. For example, is your fear related to confrontation, conflict, or someone getting mad at you? Once you know what your fear is, ask yourself how likely that outcome really is. Often, we overestimate the likelihood of negative consequences.

Additionally, ask yourself what would happen if that feared outcome did occur, and how bad would it be? And how you can handle it. This will remind you that you can get what you want without conflict, and that even when things don't go your way, you are resilient enough to handle the situation.

By challenging the negative thoughts and fears, you can focus on the actual outcome, and that will make you more confident in setting boundaries.

It's important to start working on overcoming barriers to setting boundaries as soon as possible. One way to do this is to take a moment to reflect on what your boundaries are and where they come from. Consider what you are willing and unwilling to accept in your relationships and interactions with others.

Also, take the time to identify the limiting beliefs or myths that may be holding you back from setting boundaries. Challenge these myths by reframing your thoughts and identifying the truth. Remember to remind yourself of these challenges daily, until you truly believe them.

Additionally, evaluate if you are "catastrophizing" the consequences of setting boundaries, and if so, remind yourself of the actual outcome, and that you can handle it. By starting to take these steps, you can begin to build the skills and confidence needed to effectively communicate and advocate for yourself.

Dealing With The Guilt Of Setting Boundaries

The Following Factors that Contribute to Guilt when Establishing Boundaries:

1. Selfishness and Meanness as Reasons for Guilt:

Setting boundaries is often associated with being selfish or mean. This belief is often instilled through societal or familial norms that prioritize the needs of others over one's own.

As a result, you may feel guilty for putting your own needs first. However, this is a misconception, setting boundaries is an act of self-care and compassion. By setting healthy boundaries, individuals can alleviate feelings of resentment and foster greater empathy towards others.

It's important to note that boundaries are not about denying others their needs, but about taking care of yourself and creating a healthy balance in relationships.

It's important to communicate these boundaries with respect and empathy for the other person, so that they understand that it's not about rejecting them, but about taking care of yourself.

2. The Fear of Disappointment and Backlash:

Another reason why you may feel guilty when setting boundaries is the fear of disappointing others or facing backlash. This fear often stems from the desire to be liked and accepted by others, which may lead to feeling guilty for prioritizing one's own needs.

This can manifest in over-explaining oneself or going out of one's way to justify the decision to set boundaries. However, it is important to remember that avoiding setting boundaries to avoid potential negative reactions from others is not a healthy way to maintain relationships. It is important to communicate your boundaries clearly and assertively, and not to apologize for taking care of yourself

3. The Fear of Losing Approval and Love:

Another reason you may feel guilty when setting boundaries is the fear of losing approval and love from others. This fear is often rooted in past experiences of enmeshment, where boundaries were not respected or even non-existent within the family system.

In these situations, setting boundaries may be met with resistance and accusations of selfishness, leading to feelings of guilt. It's important to remember that setting boundaries is not a choice of being selfish or not caring about others, it's about caring for yourself and setting healthy limits. It's also important to understand that setting boundaries may lead to some temporary discomfort but it's important for overall well-being and creating a healthy relationship dynamic.

The Three-Step Method for Dealing with Guilt and Regret When Setting Boundaries

Dealing with guilt and regret when setting boundaries may take some time, but with practice, these feelings will become less intense and easier to manage. The key is to consistently work through a process that addresses the underlying issues and reinforces the importance of self-care and healthy boundaries.

The key to overcoming guilt and regret when setting boundaries is to first establish clear and healthy boundaries and practice the concept of loving detachment. This process aims to shift your mindset from fear-based emotions such as anger, guilt, and regret, to love-based emotions like compassion, understanding, and kindness. By implementing this approach, you can effectively navigate the emotions that may arise when setting boundaries, and ultimately make choices that are in alignment with your personal values and well-being.

Step 1: Recognize and acknowledge your emotions when setting boundaries.

Be mindful of any feelings of guilt, shame, or regret that may arise. Preparing yourself mentally beforehand can make it easier to identify these emotions as they arise.

When someone tests your boundaries, it can be difficult to know how to react. In these situations, it's common to feel angry as a result of someone knowingly or unknowingly pushing against what we consider to be our limits.

However, it's important to recognize and acknowledge this anger instead of ignoring it or pushing it aside. One way to do this is to take a moment to notice and be present with the feeling without judgment or impatience. By acknowledging and being present with the feeling, we can better understand and address it. Additionally, it's important to remember that every thought we have creates some kind of feeling and being mindful of these emotions can help us navigate challenging situations with more clarity and self-awareness.

Step 2: Emphasize Empathy rather than Sympathy.

We get into "doing" when we feel pity for someone. If your best friend's father dies, you feel pity for them. You go into action mode and consider what you can do to help your friend's situation. You might call and check in every day, or you would cook meals. Of course, this is a great reaction.

When you've established a boundary, sympathy is NOT a healthy response. Instead, you should concentrate on empathy. This indicates you are sympathetic to and patient with the other person's situation, but you do not take it on.

Here's your top-secret method

Rather than thinking:

"What can I do to improve this?"

change your focus to

"What can I think about this?" Then take a deep breath and spend a minute adjusting your thoughts about what's going on so that you may arrive from a caring, empathic place.

Below are some boundaries setting Matras that may help when you when you are struggle or feeling guilty:

Setting limits is both kind and compassionate.

Setting limits allows others to see the real me.

My boundaries are sound and do not require explanation.

In this moment, I feel compassion for both of us.

I'm creating boundaries because I care about this person.

Emotions are not facts. This sense of guilt is an old one. My new perspective is that it is healthy to feel sympathy for this individual rather than resentment.

I am not responsible for the feelings of others.

It is not my obligation to make them feel at ease. It is solely my obligation to treat myself and others with kindness.

Step 3: Stand firm with "Yes, and"

When you establish your boundary with love, you will feel different because you will receive a different response, which will allow you to avoid feeling guilty.

When you react from a position of fear, you'll get into an emotional struggle with the other person's reaction (when you're afraid, they'll be afraid). So, as a result, DO NOT:

Ever apologize for establishing and maintaining a boundary.

Argue

Justify

Explain

Request clarification or permission.

say "but"

Instead, It's a "yes, and...". In practice, this can look like:

I can tell you're sad that I won't be joining you.

You appear to be upset that I won't be able to assist you on Saturday. I understand, and please give me a month's notice in the future, and I'll do my best to assist.

I'm intrigued by what you're saying, but I'm not sure that will work.

Remember that you have no control over their reactions. It is your responsibility to ensure that you are being kind, patient, and even loving when you express your needs.

The Ten Laws Of Boundaries

1.　　The Law of Sowing and Reaping

The idea behind the phrase "You will reap what you sow" is that the actions and choices we make will ultimately determine the outcomes we experience. This applies not only to our personal actions and decisions, but also to the way we interact with others.

Setting clear and consistent boundaries in our relationships can help us achieve positive results, both in our interactions with others and in our overall well-being. By being clear about what we are willing and not willing to accept in our relationships, we create a sense of clarity and predictability that can lead to greater peace and satisfaction.

Additionally, by consistently enforcing these boundaries and holding ourselves and others accountable, we can create healthier, more fulfilling relationships.

2. The Law of Responsibility

You hold the key to your own happiness and well-being. By setting boundaries that safeguard your emotions and physical well-being, you open the door to a greater sense of peace and contentment. Remember, you are in charge of your life, and it is your choice to determine what you want. Establishing clear boundaries allows you to take control and make choices that align with your values and aspirations. Embrace your power to shape your own happiness and well-being.

3. The Law of Respect

Respecting one another's boundaries is a crucial aspect of healthy relationships. By valuing and honoring each other's boundaries, we foster a sense of mutual respect and understanding. This leads to greater harmony, trust, and intimacy in our relationships. When we respect and are respected, we create an environment of mutual support and growth.

4. The Law of Motivation

We are naturally inclined to take action towards things that align with our values and goals. Setting boundaries that reflect these values and goals, not only helps us to maintain them but also increases our motivation to do so.

When our boundaries align with our aspirations, we feel a sense of purpose and drive to uphold them. By creating boundaries that are meaningful and important to us, we are more likely to stay committed and motivated to maintain them. It's important to find the balance between setting boundaries that are important to us and being open to other perspectives and possibilities. This will help us to maintain our boundaries and achieve our aspirations.

5. The Law of Envy

Envy arises when we lack clear boundaries. It can make us feel resentful and deprived, robbing us of clarity and peace.

By setting clear boundaries, we can reduce feelings of envy and create a sense of clarity and peace in our lives. Clear boundaries help us to understand and accept our own limitations and aspirations, and to respect the same in others. By having a clear understanding of what we want and what we are willing to accept, we can reduce feelings of envy and resentment. Establishing boundaries helps us to stay true to ourselves and our values, leading to a more peaceful and fulfilled life.

6. The Law of Evaluation

Maintaining healthy and balanced relationships require effort and regular evaluation. Setting boundaries and regularly assessing them is a key aspect of achieving balance in our relationships. By taking the time to evaluate our relationships, we can ensure that they align with our values and goals.

Regularly checking in on the health of our relationships allows us to make adjustments and changes as needed, leading to more harmony, trust, and intimacy. By actively working to maintain healthy and balanced relationships, we can experience deeper connections and more fulfilling interactions with those we care about.

7. The Law of Proactivity

Taking control of our lives and choices is crucial for our well-being. By setting boundaries and taking responsibility for our actions, we empower ourselves to make choices that best suit us. This leads to a greater sense of control and peace in our lives. By being accountable for our actions, we can learn from our mistakes, grow, and improve.

Setting boundaries enables us to define our own space and make choices that are in alignment with what we want. Being in charge of our own lives and taking responsibility for our choices is the foundation of self-empowerment, which leads to inner peace and satisfaction.

8. The Law of Activity

We must take action to bring about change. Setting boundaries and taking action to maintain them will lead to positive changes in our life and relationships.

9. The Law of Exposure

The people we surround ourselves with have a significant impact on who we become. By setting boundaries we attract people who share similar values and aspirations. This leads to a sense of alignment and support in our relationships, as well as a greater likelihood of achieving our goals.

When we surround ourselves with like-minded individuals, we gain a sense of belonging and support that helps us to grow and evolve. Setting boundaries and aligning them with our values and goals, helps us to build a community of people who will support and encourage us in our pursuits.

10. The Law Of Power

The law of power states that we have the power to choose our attitudes and actions, and we are responsible for the consequences of those choices. This principle can help us set boundaries by reminding us that we are in control of our own actions and reactions, and that we have the ability to make choices that will lead to a clearer and more peaceful life.

By setting boundaries, we are taking ownership of our own lives and taking responsibility for our own well-being. We are saying that we have the power to decide what is best for us, and we will not allow others to dictate our choices or control our behavior. This can lead to a sense of empowerment and self-confidence that can help us navigate difficult situations and relationships.

The law of power also reminds us that we are responsible for the consequences of our choices, which can help us make more thoughtful and intentional decisions.

The law of power in the context of boundaries can help us establish and maintain clear, healthy boundaries that lead to greater clarity and peace in our lives.

How To Set Boundaries

What are boundaries?

Boundaries are lines that define the limits of an area, whether that be physical or within a relationship. They serve as a means of setting guidelines and rules for how one should be treated and how one will respond when those boundaries are not respected. Essentially, boundaries help establish healthy and respectful interactions.

So first, ask yourself who or what is causing unnecessary stress in your life or who or what is draining your energy. I tell most of my clients that if they don't address this issue, it will be difficult to set boundaries, and I guess that's what you don't want.

You must become aware of what is causing you unnecessary stress; you have to decide what are the things that are not beneficial to you and your space. Or who or what is not beneficial in your space. You must determine if something serves you or not. You must determine if their energy serves you and how it serves you.

Check out the people in your space and know if they are actually bringing positive or negative energy to the kingdom; in science, there's this term called sieving; sieving is used to differentiate between good and bad substances.

You must apply that same principle to your life and everything around you. This might be in your workplace, home, neighborhood, etc.; you have to pick out the people or things causing you a high-stress level. Sometimes it might be something or someone dear to you, but you have to look beyond that and create that boundary to have clarity. Have you realized how you tend to deliver and perform when stressed? So, to stop underperforming, make deliberate action to identify the things that are causing you stress.

As individuals with differences, we need to identify our specific stress triggers. We all respond to things differently and that's because of our unique personalities and perspectives.

Your stress triggers will be different from others, so it's important to identify your own stress triggers.

For those of you who are in a toxic relationship, you know that your partner is causing you the most stress, and your mental wellness is being compromised daily, while you are hoping for the situation to change. Most situations don't get better; it definitely doesn't get better without setting clear precise boundaries.

Many people die in silence because they continue compromising on their feelings, hoping that the situation will get better. Stress can kill you. So why would you allow anything or anybody to keep stressing the hell out of you? Do you want to lose your sanity? Most mental breakdowns are caused by stress-related issues. So, start telling yourself the truth.

Also, look at the things that make you feel safe or at peace. Once this is determined, decide how you want to allow people or things in your life that have crossed the boundaries based on what makes you feel safe or at peace.

As you set the boundary, you should also know to take note of the things that have brought you peace most of the time and give them more access to your space so your peace level can increase.

Never compromise on the things that interfere with your peace of mind.

The second step is to openly communicate the boundaries that have been crossed and the line you intend to create after you have identified the things causing you the most stress and pain. There has to be clear and open communication with the person you are setting boundaries with. It is important you be prepared when having that conversation with the person.

You have to understand that having that conversation with the person you are setting the boundaries with will be difficult because the person may not want to hear you out due to selfish interests and desires. You must let them know that you have set the boundaries and will not compromise with them or the boundaries.

And you have to be ready for that uncomfortable conversation with yourself and the person involved.

Creating boundaries is almost always uncomfortable for the person setting them and with whom it's being set for.

The chances are slim that the person you are setting the boundary with is going to adhere.

Why? because they are used to crossing the line with you.

If creating a boundary will be uncomfortable, then communicating that boundary will be even more uncomfortable.

I want people to see that the things that they struggle with are the things that can help them be stronger later in life. So, if you're reading this book and struggling with the boundary setting process. I have the solution for you; email me and book a Level Up session with me so that I can show you how you can communicate boundaries just the way I did in my own life.

You may be comfortable with any one of the steps in the boundary setting process. And that's ok, it's complex for beginners, and that's why I am here to help you out. Don't allow your fears of getting it wrong to hold you back. All you need to do is take action. I can help you with the rest of the process. Now I want you to go through the boundary process again and identify which step you are struggling with. That is a sign that you need help, which is why I am there to guide you.

And remember If you haven't communicated the boundary, the other person doesn't even know that the boundary exists. It's just an imaginary line that only you are aware of; in your mind, you have created the boundary, and in the other person's mind, they have no idea the boundary exists. This will be an epic fail.

We must be able to communicate clearly, and honestly about what we want and don't want; no matter how uncomfortable it is, we must be willing to do that.

The brain hates new things, so it will always try to take you back to what is comfortable. So, if you set the boundary, you will have to keep the boundary and stand firm with it. And don't forget to determine what the consequence will be if the person crosses the boundary.

This could be determined by who, and what the situation is. For instance, if a coworker vs. a friend crosses the boundary, you can't possibly choose the same consequence for both. The consequences you will set for a friend will be totally different from that of a co-worker. This is one reason why it is important to determine the consequence at the moment the boundary is set.

Determine the consequences early on; you don't want to wait until after the person has crossed the line before you start thinking of the consequence. You must be prepared ahead of time.

Express your needs in a relaxed, loving way; remember boundaries are set out of love for self and others. Now let me tell you why you need to have that open conversation with them.

You need to have that open conversation with them to inform them about the changes you've made to your space that they are not aware of, and the consequences attached if they fail to abide by it.

Thirdly, you must be consistent with your message

It's your sole responsibility to uphold the boundaries. This will be new for everyone, including you. Initially this may not go over well. And remember you will be tested.

Setting boundaries takes repetition and patience. You don't just set boundaries and go back and sit down.

When setting boundaries, it's important to consistently remind others of them. Even if you face rejection, like being denied a job you're passionate about, it's important to stay persistent and not compromise. Constantly reminding others of your boundaries will make them understand that you are serious about them.

If someone doesn't respect your boundaries, don't change the boundaries; change how the person is in your space. You don't have to be hard on yourself if someone doesn't respect the boundary you set, and if they don't respect it, revoke their access to your space. Chickie, this is your life; the universe gave you this life to do great things with, so you can't let anyone interfere with your life purpose.

Now let's analyze this example. Imagine that you get employed at a job, and the company gives you its rules and regulations. They find out that you can't follow rules and regulations. Will the company change their rules and regulations because of you? Not at all; they will not do that; instead, they will lay you off. And that is precisely what you need to do.

When you notice someone in your space is not respecting your boundaries and causing stress, remove them before they contaminate your space with toxicity and negative energy.

Do you know that if you keep those people in your space, you will unconsciously start acting like them? According to psychology, we are a sum total of the people we hang around with, the books we read, the videos we watch, and the things we hear. if they cannot respect the boundary you have set, please let them go.

If you don't let them, go, you won't be open to meeting new people who vibrate at the same frequency as you, so when you let them go, the universe will see that you're no longer having anything to do with negativity and toxicity. The universe will send people to you who think and act in a way that is similar to yours.

There is a popular saying we all are familiar with "The best way to move forward is to let go of the people holding you back. I promise chickie, if you let go of the toxic people in your life, you're guaranteed to move forward creating a space for new people with a positive mindset and a toxic free way of life.

I've met plenty of women besides myself who took their life from zero to hero. And what I've noticed is that there is one thing consistent in their life, and that is "Change". I want you to also notice that these women are very particular about the people they have in their circle. For the most part it's positive, high vibrational, and like-minded people inspiring them to attain greater heights.

So, you see why you don't need to compromise. And you have to also know that these boundaries you are setting are for yourself, and it is to protect yourself and your space. So, don't feel too emotional about it if you feel as if you're being selfish or mean, don't buy into that, please.

We are conditioned to feel guilty when we think about our needs before others. We're born with loving hearts that can accommodate excess. It is our responsibility to control the volume of excesses we accommodate.

This journey is not going to be perfect, and that is okay. There will be times that will seem as if you are pushing everyone out of your life. When you are feeling this way, remind yourself that you must be aware of what is affecting your peace.

Set aside your weekly "me-time." Self-care is not selfish despite what we've been taught. Caring for ourselves must take place to continue in greatness. Pouring into yourself is a boundary that you create with yourself; that shows you respect and care for your kingdom as well. You cannot expect others to respect your space if you are not doing so first.

Without Boundaries, there is chaos, and where there is chaos, there is fogginess and uncertainty. Creating boundaries removes the chaos and fogginess from our lives, creating a path of clarity.

As human beings, we all need some sense of structure and order in our lives. Without boundaries, things can quickly spiral out of control, leaving us feeling lost, confused, and unsure of ourselves. It's like navigating through a dense fog with no clear direction or destination.

But when we set boundaries, we can create a sense of clarity and purpose in our lives. By establishing limits and communicating our needs and wants effectively, we can take control of our own lives and make decisions that align with our values and goals.

Think of it this way, without boundaries, we're like a ship without a rudder, drifting aimlessly on the sea. But when we set boundaries, we can chart a course and steer ourselves in the direction we want to go.

Setting boundaries is essential for caring for ourselves and ensuring we treat ourselves with love and respect. Remember: The first boundary we should set is for ourselves by implementing a self-care routine. We can't expect others to care for us if we're not taking care of ourselves first. It's like building a house; you must lay a strong foundation before building the rest.

Self-care can mean different things to different people; for some, it could be going to the gym three times a week, getting a massage, or doing an hour of meditation every day. Whatever it is, it's essential to make time for yourself and to let others see that you're taking care of yourself. By doing this, you're showing others that you respect yourself, and this is your expectation of others.

Taking care of ourselves also brings clarity and peace to our lives. We can think more clearly and make better decisions when we feel good.

So, setting boundaries for self-care is important for ourselves and our overall well-being and happiness.

In short, setting boundaries for self-care is essential for treating ourselves with love and respect and creating a foundation for others to do the same. Self-care is the first boundary you should set, and it's essential to make time for yourself and let others see that you're making you a priority. This will bring clarity and peace to your life helping you to be more relaxed and productive.

Also, remember that setting boundaries and practicing self-care is not selfish; it is self-love. It's important to remember that taking care of yourself is not a luxury; it's a necessity. It's a way of showing respect and love for yourself and valuing your needs and well-being.

Incorporating self-care into your daily routine can be difficult, especially if you're not use to it. But it's worth it; it's like planting a seed, it takes time and effort to grow, but with patience and consistency, it will flourish. Start small with something manageable and make it a habit.

And as time goes on, you will see the positive effects of self-care in your life.

Furthermore, setting boundaries for self-care also helps to establish healthy boundaries in other areas of your life, such as work, relationships, and personal growth. When you respect yourself and your own needs, it becomes easier to communicate them, which helps establish healthy relationships and professional boundaries.

Setting boundaries for self-care is essential for treating ourselves with love and respect, creating a foundation for others to do the same, and achieving clarity and peace in our lives. Remember, self-care is not selfish, it's self-love, and it's essential for our overall well-being and happiness. So, make sure to incorporate self-care into your daily routine and see its positive effects on your life.

Setting Boundaries with families

Boundaries have become a popular topic on social media, with many posts and memes dedicated to the subject. Some of these may offer valuable insights, while others may promote avoidance of personal responsibility.

With the nation being divided on many issues and perspectives on boundaries also being diverse, it's important to consider the best way to set boundaries with family members, especially when it comes to toxic family members. Setting boundaries with friends or romantic partners may seem straightforward, but dealing with family can be much more complicate

Here's how to set boundary with your families

1. Value yourself and your time.

It is vital to understand your worth and to be treated accordingly. If the people in your life, whether they are family or not, fail to show appreciation and respect towards you, it is important to question the value of spending time with them.

You have the power to make choices about who you spend time with, and when, and it is essential to recognize that your time is valuable. If you do not value your time, it is unlikely that anyone else will either.

Make a conscious effort to surround yourself with individuals who uplift and support you, rather than those who bring negativity and harm. Imagine the positive impact it would have on your life if you only spent time with people who truly care for and value you.

2. Give yourself permission to do what's best for you.

Society often dictates that we should spend a significant amount of time with our family, particularly during holidays, and that not doing so is a sign of something being amiss.

However, if your family is toxic, and familial relationships are harmful, it is essential to remember that you are your own best advocate and supporter. Having healthy boundaries, regardless of whether or not others understand or accept them, is crucial for self-care. Limiting time with toxic individuals, whether family or not, is an act of self-love and should not be stigmatized. You are allowed to prioritize your well-being and mental health.

3. Know your triggers and anticipate them.

Each of us has different things that can trigger us emotionally. These triggers can range from small actions or events, such as a family member's behavior, to more significant experiences.

To manage your triggers, it is essential to be aware of them and understand the emotions they evoke. It is also important to have a plan in place for how to care for yourself and respond when triggered. To prepare for a potentially triggering situation, consider practicing with a friend, including how to exit the conversation calmly and leave. By being proactive and prepared, you can minimize the stress of a triggering situation.

4. **Be clear about your needs and communicate them.**

It's important to identify your needs and boundaries in advance, such as how much time you want to spend with family, friends, or alone. For example, you may set boundaries around when your mother-in-law visits, or if you would prefer that she leaves her pet at home.

It's also important to remember that it's okay to not want to spend time with your family during the holidays and instead choose to spend time with friends.

It's important to remember that it's your life and your time, and you have the right to make decisions about your relationships, even if it is painful. To make sure your needs and boundaries are respected, it's crucial to communicate them clearly and kindly.

5. **Practice saying no.**

It's important to practice saying no, especially if you are someone who finds it difficult to disappoint others. Saying no can be especially challenging when it comes to family. Some "no's" are easier to say than others, such as "soft no's" which leave room for a potential "yes" in the future, while "hard no's" are firm and definitive.

One strategy to practice saying no is to create a "menu" of different ways to say no, ranging from the softest to the hardest and practice them in different scenarios until it feels familiar and comfortable.

Through practice, you can become better at advocating for yourself and setting limits. This not only helps you feel stronger and more self-confident but also communicates to others that you know your needs and are not afraid to state them. Setting boundaries is beneficial for relationships, not harmful, even if it feels uncomfortable at first.

6.   Make a list of coping strategies.

It is helpful to have a list of coping strategies in place before a potentially triggering event. These strategies can include physical activities such as going for a walk, taking a bath, or lifting weights, as well as mindfulness practices like deep breathing, meditation, or journaling.

Other options can be listening to calming music, talking to a designated friend, or joining an online support group. You can also consider self-care activities such as getting a massage or watching a movie. In some cases, it may be best to skip the event altogether and opt for an escape like heading to Mexico. Having a list of coping strategies in advance will help you navigate through a triggering situation and take care of yourself.

How To Set Boundaries With Friends?

Boundaries are not only essential for self-care but also for maintaining healthy relationships. While some boundaries may be established at the beginning of a friendship, others may need to be established as the relationship evolves over time.

This can be challenging as it often means asking a friend to make changes to their behavior or communication. However, creating new boundaries can be crucial for maintaining the emotional well-being of both parties involved in the relationship. It may be difficult, but it is important for preserving healthy and fulfilling friendships.

If you are facing issues in a friendship, it may be a sign that there are unmet needs or lack of communication around boundaries. Instead of immediately ending the friendship, try setting new boundaries as a way to address the problem. Having boundaries in a friendship is not only about saying no, but also about managing the space and communication between you and the other person. It's about opening and closing doors and windows, instead of building walls. It's important to try to navigate the relationship and find a way to make it work.

Common reasons for boundary setting with friends

1. You are overwhelmed and underwater

In normal times, we may have a few friends who need support at a given moment, but these days, it can feel like everyone is in need of help, while we are struggling too. It can be difficult to navigate this situation as it may feel uncomfortable to tell a friend that you are unable to support them right now. However, it is important to remember that you need to prioritize your own needs and well-being.

It's essential to understand that you can't pour from an empty cup. Given the current national and global circumstances, many of us are feeling drained. In such situations, you can communicate to your friend that you want to support them, but you don't have the energy to do so in the way that they deserve at the moment, and that's why it's better to refer them to a support group or therapist or other coping strategies that don't require much emotional energy.

You can also let them know that this is a temporary boundary due to the extraordinary circumstances, and not a permanent shift.

2. Your availability has changed

Even in normal times, it's possible for a friend to ask for more than what you are able or willing to give. For instance, if you're going through a phase in life where you have other demands that are taking up most of your time and energy, such as having children, you may not be able to devote the same level of time or resources to your friend as you did before.

3. The relationship is too one-sided

It's normal for friendships to require new boundaries when they become unbalanced. When one person is giving significantly more than the other, it may be necessary to set a boundary to prevent one person from feeling like they're not getting the benefit that

they should from the friendship. The aim of setting
such a boundary is to achieve a mutually beneficial
relationship.

4. You don't feel safe to share

Boundaries of trust are essential for a healthy
friendship. It's important to be able to trust that you
can share personal information with a friend and
that it will not be shared with others. Trust is often
the foundation of a friendship, but if it's broken, it
may be necessary to establish boundaries around
what you are willing to share moving forward or
what your expectations are for keeping confidences
in the future.

5. You don't appreciate their teasing

In close friendships, it can happen that one person
may not be aware of the other person's feelings or
sensitivities. This may require setting boundaries on
the way jokes or teasing are made, particularly if it's
at the expense of one person's feelings.

6. You have different communication styles

Different people have different preferences when it comes to communication, some prefer texting while others might be more comfortable with calls.

If you find that the mode of communication that a friend consistently uses causes you stress, it might be necessary to set a boundary and communicate your preference for a different mode of communication.

7. You feel like you're always on call

You may also need to set a boundary around your availability through text or phone. If you feel that someone has an expectation that you should always be available and respond immediately, it's important to set a new expectation of your availability.

How to set the boundaries with the friend

1. Open a dialogue

Before taking any drastic action such as cutting off communication, it's important to have a conversation with your friend about the relationship dynamic and express your concerns. Explain what is bothering you and how you would like things to change, and also ask your friend for their perspective. Instead of acting on a new boundary without discussing it, it's important to address the dynamic first and have a conversation before making any changes.

2. Be explicit

In order to establish effective boundaries, it is important to be able to clearly communicate the problem. Instead of making general statements, it's better to be specific and give clear instructions on what needs to change. For example, instead of saying "stop acting like everything is about you", it would be better to say "I need you to listen to me more often instead of doing all the talking" as this gives the person a clear direction on how to improve the situation.

3. Nip the problematic behavior in the bud as early as possible

Act quickly to address problematic behavior as soon as it arises. Don't wait until the situation escalates and becomes unbearable before setting boundaries. It may be challenging to confront the issue early on, but it's better than dealing with the aftermath of a major argument or fight.

4. Use "I" statements

When discussing boundaries with a friend, focus on how their behavior makes you feel, instead of just pointing out their problem. Instead of saying "you're being overwhelming or aggressive" say "I feel uncomfortable" or "I'm feeling nervous about expressing myself in this relationship." The key is to communicate your internal experience and share it with them so they can understand and meet your needs, rather than diagnosing or telling them what to do. Remember that setting boundaries is not about punishing them, but it's about addressing your own needs.

5. Emphasize the value of your friendship

Even when communicated in a gentle manner, setting boundaries can still come across as hurtful, especially in long-term friendships. To make it less confrontational, stress how much the relationship means to you and that you're having this conversation because you value the friendship. This will make it clear that you are willing to work through the issues instead of just walking away from the relationship.

6. Offer alternatives

Another way to make the transition to new boundaries easier is by offering an alternative to what you were previously providing in the friendship. For instance, if your new boundary is not responding to messages immediately, you can propose a scheduled phone call as a replacement. This way, you're still meeting their needs but in a different way.

7. Consider a compromise

In certain situations, you may need to compromise with your friend as their boundaries could be conflicting with yours. An example could be if you prefer phone communication and they prefer text, you both have to find a solution that works for both of you. Or in the case of a roommate, if you need them to do the dishes to maintain the living arrangements and they despise doing dishes, you may have to come to an agreement and swap chores, where you take on the laundry and they handle the dishes.

8. Be assertive

It's important to be considerate while setting boundaries, keeping in mind the feelings of the other person, but at the same time, you should be assertive and make sure they understand that you are serious about the boundaries you're trying to establish. If you downplay your need for the boundary, you may find yourself having to continuously reinforce it or feeling frustrated that it's not being respected.

What to do if the friend doesn't respect your requested boundaries

1. Outline consequences

It's important to establish and enforce consequences when someone disregards your boundaries. Without consequences, boundaries can easily be disregarded and seen as mere suggestions.

For example, if a roommate repeatedly borrows your clothes without permission, it would be appropriate to inform them that if it continues, the ultimate consequence could be finding a new place to live.

It's important to phrase the consequence in a way that allows them to make a choice and avoid defensiveness. Additionally, it's essential to follow through on any consequences communicated, therefore, it's best to propose consequences that you are willing and able to enforce.

2. Avoid situations where the boundary comes up

In some cases, despite clear communication, the other person may not be willing to respect your boundaries. In these situations, rather than ending the friendship, it may be necessary to accept that there may be certain activities or situations that are no longer compatible with the friendship.

For example, if your friend likes to talk while you're trying to watch TV, and it's something you can't tolerate, it might be better to avoid engaging in that activity together. The key is to find a compromise that allows the friendship to continue without compromising your own boundaries.

3. Consider moving on from the friendship

Establishing new boundaries in an existing relationship can be challenging as it may change the dynamics of the relationship. If the boundary you set is significant, it may not be possible for the friendship to adapt to it. It's important to remember that relationships function within the boundaries that are currently in place.

Therefore, setting new boundaries may lead to the end of the relationship. While this can be difficult, it's important to remember that staying in a relationship that no longer serves you is not healthy.

A healthy relationship is one in which boundaries
that are healthy for you are respected and upheld.

Setting Boundaries With A Spouse

In relationships, having clear boundaries is essential for defining what actions and behaviors are acceptable to you and what you expect from your partner. While the idea of "unconditional love" may seem appealing, it can actually be detrimental to the health of the relationship if it leads to accepting any and all behavior from your partner without question. Setting boundaries allows you to assert your own needs and wants while also fostering mutual respect and understanding in the relationship.

"The foundation of a healthy relationship lies in the establishment of clear boundaries and mutual respect for them. Without these, the relationship is likely to suffer."

Leigh McInnis, LPC

Types Of Boundaries In Relationships

Different types of boundaries exist in relationships to ensure each partner's needs and limitations are respected. These can include:

Emotional boundaries

Which safeguard each individual's right to have their own thoughts, feelings, and values without being belittled or invalidated.

Intellectual boundaries

That protects each partner's right to have their own thoughts, opinions, and beliefs without being judged or criticized.

Physical boundaries

Which help define personal space and preferences around physical touch, as well as physical needs such as rest, food, and water.

Sexual boundaries

Which encompass partners' needs and limitations in terms of sexual interactions, including what type of contact is or isn't comfortable and when and where intimacy is appropriate.

Time boundaries

Which involves respecting each other's time and setting limits on how often you spend time together and how you'd like to spend it.

Communication boundaries

Which can be set to manage conflicts or arguments, such as avoiding name-calling or bringing up past arguments.

Material boundaries

Which relate to personal possessions and finances, and the degree to which you are comfortable sharing these with your partner.

Benefits Of Setting Boundaries In A Relationship

Setting boundaries in a relationship has several benefits, including:

Preserving individuality

By establishing healthy boundaries, you and your partner can maintain your distinct identities, thoughts, and feelings, promoting autonomy and self-respect.

Fostering respect

Setting firm boundaries is essential for gaining your partner's respect and building a healthy relationship, as mutual respect is a key ingredient for a successful relationship.

Avoiding manipulation

Clear boundaries can protect you from being manipulated or taken advantage of and help you to assert yourself and your preferences.

Establishing expectations

By setting boundaries, you and your partner can outline your responsibilities and expectations within the relationship, helping to create a sense of security and understanding.

Building closeness

Ultimately, setting boundaries in a relationship can help you and your partner communicate your needs and preferences to each other, fostering a greater sense of comfort and intimacy within the relationship.

How To Set Boundaries With Your Spouse?

Clarifying your own boundaries

Before communicating them to your partner, it's important to take the time to fully understand your own boundaries. Reflecting on what you're comfortable with and what you're not can aid in identifying and communicating your boundaries effectively.

Pay Close Attention To The Boundary Set By Your Spouse

It is crucial to give heed to the boundaries set by your significant other as effective communication involves not only expressing oneself, but also attentively listening to one's partner. Take the time to truly listen to each other to guarantee that you fully comprehend their boundaries. If needed, don't hesitate to inquire for further explanation to clarify any confusion.

Understand That You deserve To Be Respected:

It is crucial to show love, compassion, kindness, and respect towards your partner, but it is also imperative to remember that you deserve the same level of treatment in return. Ensure that your partner is treating you with the respect you deserve.

Point Out The Things That Makes You Uncomfortable

It's vital to be vocal when your partner's actions or words cause discomfort to you. Expressing yourself and letting them know that they have overstepped a boundary is important for them to understand and avoid similar behavior in the future.

Setting Boundaries With Children

As a parent, it's important to be aware of when your child is overstepping boundaries. Here are a few examples:

Your teenager enters your room without first knocking and disregards your personal space.

Your pre-teen interrupts your conversations with other adults without the proper etiquette of saying "excuse me" or waiting for an appropriate moment.

Your adolescent child gives you unsolicited advice on how to handle your personal life after a divorce.

Your child throws temper tantrums and demands you to do what she says.

Crossing boundaries can be a subtle or obvious experience. It can manifest in various ways, such as feeling uneasy, irritated, uncomfortable, resentful, ashamed, or taken advantage of. You may also experience a sense of loss of control or feeling as if you are in an inappropriate situation.

It could also be seen in your child behaving in a way that is not appropriate for their age or role, such as giving unsolicited advice about your relationship, personal life or acting as if they are the authority. It's essential to learn how to set and maintain healthy boundaries and understand your respective roles as a parent.

Want to establish strong boundaries with your children? Here are a few suggestions that can assist you in achieving this goal:

1. Clearly establish your boundaries

To effectively set boundaries with your children, it is essential to understand your own values, beliefs, and convictions. This process may not always be easy, but it is crucial for your children to know who you are and what you stand for.

This does not mean being inflexible, but rather expressing your personal values and adhering to them. For example, if honesty is a value, you hold dear, it's crucial to not only speak about it but also demonstrate it through your actions. Children tend to learn more from observing than from listening to what's being said.

2. Communicate Your Expectations:

Make a list of what you expect from your children. Identify what you can and cannot tolerate. Reflect on what values are most important to you - responsibility, loyalty, respect, etc. It may be beneficial to write it down. Clearly convey your guiding principles to your children.

Understand that by creating this list, you are not trying to control your child, but rather taking ownership of yourself. For example, if one of your values is respect and your son is often disrespectful and uses offensive language towards you, explain the consequences that will follow his behavior.

Let him see that you have self-respect and that you will follow through with the consequences. This approach differs from trying to force him to talk the way you want, instead, you are giving him the choice, but holding him accountable for his actions.

3. Focus on Yourself rather than your Child's behavior:

When your child is behaving poorly and not paying attention to you, focus on how you can communicate your expectations more effectively and hold them accountable for not listening. Speak in a way that shows that you are serious and expect to be heard and taken seriously.

It may be challenging to look at yourself honestly, but it will help you stop trying to control your child, which is futile. Instead, it will enable you to take charge of yourself. By doing so, you will continue to grow and develop, and your own self-awareness and maturity will guide your children to find their own.

4. Make your child understand the effects of crossing boundaries:

Acknowledge when you have crossed someone's boundaries and apologize for it. In the same way, when your child crosses a boundary, make them aware of it and hold them responsible for it. For instance, if you promise your child that you will take him to the movies after he finishes his chores, but he chooses to play video games instead.

If you stick to your promise and don't take him, he will experience the consequences and understand your expectations. Your child will learn that you respect yourself and you mean what you say. Over time, he will also learn to set healthy boundaries for himself and to respect others boundaries as well.

Setting boundaries with yourself

Part of being a responsible adult is setting boundaries with ourselves. We need limits to keep ourselves safe and healthy. Boundaries are guidelines and limits that are an integral part of being a responsible adult– making choices that are in our own best interest even when they aren't enjoyable at the moment.

Why you need boundaries for yourself

Boundaries play a crucial role in maintaining a healthy and balanced lifestyle. They help regulate our behavior and create structure in our lives. Setting a boundary with ourselves means drawing a line between what is acceptable and not, for example, not eating French fries every meal or staying up too late when you have to wake up early for work. By setting boundaries for ourselves, we are showing self-love and self-respect. Boundaries keep us safe and healthy and help keep our lives running smoothly.

Examples of boundaries that may be beneficial to set for yourself:

- Maintaining a budget
- Setting a daily limit on the amount of television you watch
- Keeping electronic devices out of the bedroom
- Refraining from participating in gossip or speaking ill of others behind their backs
- Establishing a cut-off time for work-related tasks
- Not responding to work emails during off hours
- Adhering to a shopping list and avoiding impulsive purchases
- Keeping a consistent sleep schedule
- Setting aside designated time for household chores
- Deciding on a specific number of dates before engaging in sexual activity

- Avoiding the urge to check social media constantly
- Limiting the frequency of eating out
- Maintaining a regular personal hygiene routine
- Avoiding people or situations that are toxic or cause stress
- Refraining from consuming alcohol during weekdays
- Avoiding keeping unhealthy food items in your home
- Setting a limit on the amount of coffee you consume daily

Keep in mind that these are just examples and that each person's boundaries will differ according to their personal needs and preferences.

Why is it difficult to set boundaries with yourself?

Many people find it challenging to set and maintain boundaries with themselves. While it is understood that having structure and limits in our lives is beneficial, sticking to them can be difficult. It's important to reflect on why it's hard for you to set boundaries for yourself. Some common reasons why it might be challenging include:

- Growing up without healthy boundaries or limits set by parents
- Having inconsistent or unrealistic boundaries set by parents during childhood
- Feeling restricted or controlled by setting boundaries
- Certain mental health conditions or addiction can make it difficult to monitor and regulate oneself.

If you were fortunate, you may have had a parent who instilled healthy habits and practices in you, such as maintaining good personal hygiene and keeping a regular sleep schedule. Through observing and internalizing these boundaries, you are now able to set them for yourself.

Setting boundaries leads to a more predictable and structured life, promoting a sense of security. Additionally, you have learned the importance of self-care and how to make choices that promote well-being.

However, for many individuals, their parents may have not set a good example of maintaining boundaries, such as engaging in unhealthy habits like chain-smoking, excessive drinking, overspending, or having frequent romantic partners.

Furthermore, in some cases, parents may have not set boundaries for their children, or if they did, it was done in an inconsistent manner. This lack of guidance and understanding can make it challenging for individuals to establish and maintain boundaries for themselves in the present.

Establishing boundaries for oneself is a way of providing yourself with the guidance, stability, and structure that may have been missing during childhood. Setting limits can help in "re-parenting" oneself, providing the necessary foundation for a healthy and well-balanced life.

Now that you understand the significance of setting boundaries with oneself, as well as some of the difficulties that may arise, you can start working on implementing the boundaries that you require.

How To Set Boundaries For Yourself?

The following suggestions can assist you in getting started:

Step 1

To begin setting boundaries for yourself, the first step is to identify the various aspects of your life that require structure or limits. Some examples may include:

- Financial management
- Interpersonal relationships
- Electronics usage
- Daily routine and habits
- Physical and emotional well-being
- Nutrition
- And so on.

Step 2

Once you have identified the areas of your life that require boundaries, make sure to craft boundaries that align with your goals and values.

Step 3

Avoid trying to implement too many boundaries all at once, as it can be overwhelming. Remember that setting boundaries is a gradual process and taking small steps can be more effective in the long run.

Step 4

Practice self-compassion and accountability when it comes to enforcing your boundaries. Remember that it's not realistic to expect yourself to be perfect and maintain all boundaries all the time.

Instead of being overly critical of yourself, when you struggle to uphold a boundary, take a kind and understanding approach. Being too hard on yourself can lead to feelings of shame, hopelessness, and giving up. Take the time to examine the reasons for any slip-ups, make any necessary adjustments to your boundaries and create a plan for improvement.

Step 5

Gradually implement changes. When trying to establish a new boundary, it can be helpful to make adjustments incrementally. For example, if you're trying to stop snacking at night, instead of cutting it off abruptly, try moving your cutoff time back by 15 minutes at a time until you reach your goal (no snacking after 9:00, then 8:45, and so forth).

Remember that setting boundaries for yourself is an act of self-love and self-care, even though it may not always feel comfortable at the moment.

Setting Boundaries With Work

The average full-time American worker spends a significant amount of time at work, with a 2014 Gallup poll showing that they spend 47 hours per week on the job. This means that work takes up a large portion of an adult's life, and as such, it can have a significant impact on one's overall well-being and happiness.

Properly setting boundaries at work is crucial in order to avoid stress and burnout. By setting boundaries, you can gain a better understanding of your responsibilities and expectations, which can lead to greater efficiency and satisfaction.

It's important to remember that work takes up more than a third of the typical workweek, from Monday to Friday, so setting boundaries at work should be a top priority. By establishing and sticking to clear boundaries, you can experience greater peace of mind and improved performance both at work and in your personal life.

Boundaries serve multiple functions and are essential for maintaining our well-being. They help us to define what is our responsibility and what belongs to others. They also serve to preserve our energy, both physical and emotional, and allow us to focus on our values and standards. Additionally, boundaries help us to identify our personal limits, and this is important for our self-care.
In the workplace setting, setting boundaries leads to a more efficient and pleasant experience. It is important to learn how to set and maintain clear boundaries with your boss and colleagues. This will help you to remain happy and productive in your work, which is essential for maintaining a good work-life balance and overall well-being.

When lines between management expectations, job responsibilities, communication, or other areas of work are not clearly defined, it can lead to stress and frustration for everyone involved.

This can negatively impact productivity and social dynamics in the workplace.

However, when boundaries are set clearly, it helps to establish a more effective and efficient work environment. When professional boundaries and priorities are clearly defined, everyone knows what is expected of them and how to behave.

This creates a more productive, respectful, and harmonious work environment. Without clear boundaries, there can be confusion and lack of accountability, which can lead to conflicts and a less productive work environment.

Example of workplace boundaries

A. Job roles and responsibilities

Setting boundaries in the workplace involves both the manager and the employees. The manager needs to set boundaries for their employees by clearly defining their roles and responsibilities, creating accountability, and reducing the chances of blame or excuses.

For employees, it is important to have a clear understanding of who they report to, who provides them with feedback, who makes decisions about their work, and who assigns them tasks.

With these clear boundaries in place, employees can establish and maintain their own boundaries more effectively. Examples of this include:

- Requesting not to be contacted at home after a certain time
- Setting specific hours to check work email
- Declining projects that exceed the employee's workload
- Communicating with the manager about situations that violate personal boundaries and working together to find a solution.

By setting and maintaining clear boundaries, both manager and employees can work more efficiently and effectively and have a better work-life balance.

B.   Personal Boundaries

Personal boundaries also play an important role in maintaining a healthy work-life balance. These boundaries help to separate work from personal life, and to ensure that work does not consume all of one's time and energy.

Personal boundaries can include:

- Not checking work-related emails or voicemails while at home
- Leaving work-related devices, such as laptops, at the office
- Using vacation time to disconnect from work and fully relax
- Taking time to disconnect from technology, such as avoiding social media or email during personal time.

By setting and maintaining personal boundaries, individuals can better manage their time and energy, reduce stress, and have a more fulfilling personal life. This ultimately leads to a more productive and satisfied employee.

C.   Interpersonal Boundaries

Interpersonal boundaries are also important in the workplace, they are the boundaries between co-workers and between employees and managers. These boundaries are related to factors such as tone of voice, attitudes, and the ability to focus on work even when there is a personal conflict.

It is important to establish clear boundaries in terms of conversation topics, for example, it is important to avoid discussing sensitive topics such as religion or personal matters that may offend others.

When interpersonal boundaries are not well defined, it can lead to issues such as bullying, as well as individuals being taken advantage of. This can negatively impact the work environment and productivity.

Strong interpersonal boundaries allow for a more productive and harmonious work environment, where co-workers can work together effectively without feeling uncomfortable or disrespected.

Setting Workplace Boundaries

Establishing boundaries at work is a gradual process that can be initiated at any time. It's often easier to set boundaries when starting a new job, as it's the time when basic work arrangements such as working hours, overtime, and remote working are being discussed. However, if you are already working and don't plan to change jobs in the near future, you can still establish boundaries through the following steps:

1.   Know what you want

To set effective boundaries, it's important to first identify what is most important to you. Take some time to reflect on what boundaries you need to protect your own happiness and well-being at work. Consider what activities and values give you a sense of fulfillment and satisfaction, and how you feel when you are operating at your optimal potential.

Also, pay attention to the moments when you feel frustrated, stressed, or overwhelmed, as these are indications that a boundary is being violated or needs to be established. For example, if physical fitness is important to you, schedule specific times for exercise.

If family dinners are a priority, set a boundary that you leave work at a specific time every day. Additionally, establish rules for yourself, such as only checking email before dinner and then putting away devices for the rest of the evening, to separate work and personal life, and to allow yourself to replenish your mental, emotional, and spiritual reserves.

By prioritizing your values and making time for the things that are important to you, you can set strict boundaries around working overtime or being available at all hours and maintain a healthy work-life balance.

2.   Address Boundaries Violations

It's important to address boundary violations as soon as they occur. Speak up and clearly communicate how the violation is impacting you and your ability to perform your job effectively. Bring up the violation promptly so that the person responsible understands its significance.

When discussing boundary violations, approach the conversation with compassion. Most people may not be aware that their actions are crossing a line and will appreciate being informed so they can avoid making the same mistake in the future. By addressing boundary violations in a timely and compassionate manner, you can maintain a positive work environment and continue to support yourself, your team, and your organization.

3.   Focus on concrete explanations rather than personal ones.

When setting boundaries at work, it is important to focus on concrete explanations rather than personal ones. Instead of expressing your objection in terms of your own stress or workload, explain how the request affects other projects, clients, or the bottom line of the company. For example, instead of saying "I'm really stressed" or "I have too much to do", you can say "If I spend my time on X, there won't be enough time to do Y.

It's also important to engage in a dialogue with the person making the request. Ask them to explain the reasoning behind it and explore the possibility of finding a mutually beneficial solution. This approach helps to reduce anxiety and opens the door to negotiation.

By using concrete explanations and engaging in dialogue, you can effectively set boundaries at work and maintain a positive work environment.

4.   Be ready for boundaries violations

It's important to be prepared for the possibility of someone violating your boundaries at work. One way to do this is to visualize potential boundary breaches and decide on a course of action in advance. For example, if you imagine your boss emailing you on a weekend, think about how you will respond. Will you reply immediately with the requested information, or will you wait until Monday and remind your boss of your boundary? Having a plan in place will help you to handle boundary breaches in a calm and assertive manner.

Having a plan in place ahead of time can help you to be prepared and prevent your emotions from taking over when boundaries are violated. Setting boundaries at work leads to a more clear and peaceful work environment.

It's important to remember that building boundaries is a process that requires time and practice. There may be times when boundaries are crossed or ignored. Instead of viewing these violations as negative experiences, try to see them as opportunities for growth and improvement in your boundary-setting skills.

What is the consequence of not setting boundaries?

Imagine a world where you constantly say "yes" to every request and never stand up for yourself or set limits on what you're willing to do. This may sound like a dream come true for the user and manipulators in your life. But in your reality, it can lead to many negative consequences that can harm your mental and emotional well-being, relationships, and overall quality of life.

One of the most significant consequences of not setting boundaries is forgetting how to say "no" when you need to. When you don't establish limits, you may find yourself constantly giving in to the demands and requests of others, even when it's not in your best interest. This can lead to feelings of resentment and frustration, as well as a sense of being taken advantage of.

Another consequence of not setting boundaries is difficulty not achieving personal goals.

When you're constantly putting the needs of others before your own, it can be hard to focus on your goals and aspirations. This can lead to a sense of stagnation and dissatisfaction, as well as a lack of progress in areas that are important to you.

Not setting boundaries can also harm your relationships. When you don't communicate your needs and wants effectively, it can be challenging for others to understand and respect your boundaries. This can lead to conflict, misunderstandings, and a lack of trust and intimacy in your relationships.

Additionally, not setting boundaries can lead to burnout. When you're constantly putting the needs of others before your own, you may feel exhausted and overwhelmed. This can lead to physical and emotional exhaustion and a lack of motivation and energy to pursue your goals and interests.

Not setting boundaries with yourself can lead to a lack of self-care and personal growth. Without limits, it can be hard to establish healthy habits, such as exercise and self-reflection, and to make time for things that are important to you.

This can lead to a lack of personal development and self-awareness, as well as a lack of fulfillment and satisfaction in your life.

Not setting boundaries can affect your work or professional life. When you don't establish limits in the workplace, you may constantly take on more responsibilities, even when it's not in your job description.

This can lead to increased stress and burnout, as well as a lack of job satisfaction and productivity. Additionally, not setting boundaries in a professional setting can lead to difficulty establishing and maintaining healthy relationships with coworkers and managers, negatively impacting your career advancement and job security.

Furthermore, not setting boundaries can also lead to a lack of personal privacy and autonomy. When you don't establish limits, others may feel entitled to your time, energy, and resources, leading to a lack of control over your life. This can be particularly challenging for people who struggle with assertiveness or self-esteem issues.

It's important to note that setting boundaries doesn't mean that you have to be rigid or inflexible. It's about learning to communicate your needs and wants clearly and respectfully and being willing to compromise when necessary. Setting boundaries is a continuous process that requires self-awareness, self-esteem, and assertiveness.

For instance, if you're finding it hard to set boundaries, start by identifying your own needs and wants, then think about how you can communicate them effectively to others. It may also be helpful to practice saying "no" politely but firmly. And, if you are feeling overwhelmed, take time to take care of yourself, and seek support and guidance.

Setting boundaries is an essential part of being human. It is a process of self-awareness, self-esteem, and assertiveness. Without boundaries, you may find yourself constantly giving in to the demands of others, feeling resentful, and struggling to progress in important areas. Remember, setting boundaries is not a sign of weakness; it's a sign of strength and self-respect. It's a way to take control of your life and live it on your own terms.

Testing The Boundary

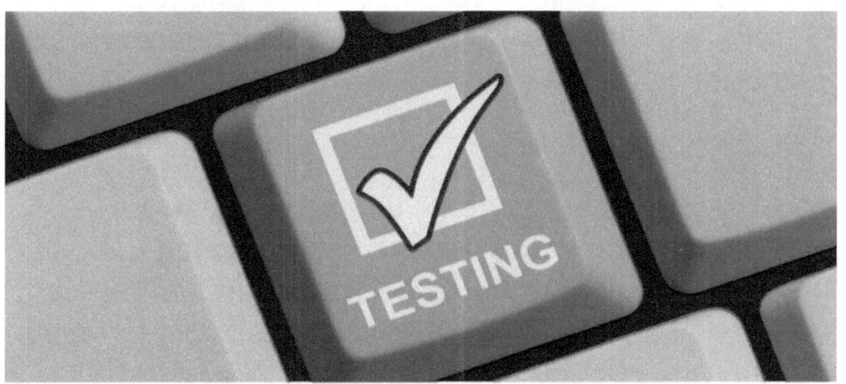

Boundaries are essential to maintaining healthy relationships, both with us and others. They are the invisible lines we draw to protect our physical, emotional, and mental well-being. But how do we know if the boundaries we set are actually working?

"The Acid Test."

The acid test is a simple yet effective way to evaluate the effectiveness of the boundaries you have set in your life. It involves observing whether or not your boundaries are being respected. Suppose the boundary is consistently being crossed or ignored. In that case, it may indicate that it is ineffective and may need to be adjusted or reinforced.

For example, if you have set a boundary with a friend to not call to discuss their personal drama after 9 pm but they continue to call and text you with their problems late at night, your boundary is not being respected.

This may be a sign that you need to have a conversation with your friend and remind them of your boundary or consider setting stricter boundaries, such as not answering calls or messages after a particular hour.

It's important to see if the boundaries are being respected by others, check in with yourself, and ensure that the boundary promotes healthy and balanced relationships with yourself and others. Feeling resentful, frustrated, or guilty after setting boundaries with others may signify that the boundary is too rigid and may need re-evaluation.

Boundaries are ongoing, and we must check in with ourselves regularly to ensure they are still serving us well. An acid test is a powerful tool that helps us to evaluate the effectiveness of the boundaries we set and adjust as necessary. Remember, setting boundaries is not about being selfish but taking care of ourselves and maintaining healthy relationships.

An acid test is a powerful tool that can help you evaluate the effectiveness of the boundaries you have set in your life. It is important to observe whether or not your boundaries are being respected and to make adjustments as necessary.

Remember to check in with yourself regularly to ensure that your boundaries promote healthy relationships and take care of yourself. Setting boundaries is crucial to maintaining healthy relationships with ourselves and others.

Boundaries are essential for creating a sense of self and maintaining healthy relationships. Setting boundaries allows individuals to define their own needs, wants, and limitations while also respecting the needs, wants, and limitations of others. When boundaries are clear and well-defined, it leads to a sense of clarity and peace.

Creating boundaries can be challenging, but it is essential to personal growth and development. It requires self-awareness, self-compassion, and the ability to communicate effectively. Self-awareness is understanding one's thoughts, feelings, and behaviors. Self-compassion is treating oneself with kindness, understanding, and respect. Effective communication is the ability to express oneself clearly and assertively.

Individuals must first identify their needs, wants, and limitations to create boundaries. This may involve taking a step back from a situation and reflecting on how it makes one feel.

Boundaries can be physical, emotional, or psychological. Physical boundaries, such as personal space, physical touch, and privacy, pertain to the body.

Emotional boundaries are those that pertain to emotions and feelings, such as the right to say no to someone's request or the right to express one's own feelings. Psychological boundaries pertain to thoughts and beliefs, such as the right to have one's own opinion or choose one's beliefs.

In conclusion, creating boundaries as a human being leads to clarity and peace. Setting boundaries allows individuals to define their own needs, wants, and limitations while also respecting the needs, wants, and limitations of others. Establishing and maintaining boundaries is an essential step in personal growth and development.

It's now time to open a new door of possibilities called "Clarity." You unlocked this door by creating boundaries around your space.

Part Two

Clarity

*"Clarity is the counterbalance of
profound thoughts"*

-

James Thurber

What Is Clarity?

Clarity refers to the state of being clear or distinct. It can refer to the quality of being easy to understand or perceive, as well as a state of being free from confusion or uncertainty. Clarity can apply to many different areas of life, such as communication, decision-making, and understanding of concepts or ideas.

In the context of personal development, clarity refers to having a clear understanding of oneself, one's values, goals and what one wants to achieve in life. Clarity in one's thoughts, emotions, and actions can lead to better decision-making, improved relationships, and overall fulfillment and satisfaction. When one is clear about what they want, they are better able to set boundaries, make choices, and take action towards achieving their goals.

Clarity can also be about finding one's own voice and being true to oneself, which can lead to self-acceptance, self-esteem, and self-love. Clarity in self-understanding and self-acceptance can help to remove self-doubt and self-criticism.

In short, clarity is the state of being clear about oneself and one's surroundings, in thoughts, emotions, and actions which can lead to better decision-making, improved relationships and overall fulfillment and satisfaction.

A day in the life of someone with clarity might look something like this

Wake up early, feeling rested and energized. Take some time to reflect on what they want to accomplish that day and set some clear goals.

Start the day with a healthy breakfast and some form of exercise, such as yoga or a morning jog.

At work, they are able to stay focused and productive, as they have a clear understanding of their tasks and priorities. They communicate effectively with their colleagues and are able to manage their time well.

During breaks and lunch, they take some time to reflect on their progress and make any necessary adjustments to their plans.

After work, they spend time with friends and family, enjoying quality time together. They are able to set clear boundaries with loved ones and have healthy and positive relationships.

Before going to bed, they review their day, reflect on what went well and what could have been better. They also take some time to plan for the next day.

They sleep well, feeling content with their day and excited for the next day.

Someone with clarity can make the most of their time, both in their professional and personal life. They can set clear goals and priorities, communicate effectively, and make decisions that align with their values and goals. They have a good understanding of themselves and what they want, and they make choices that support their personal growth and development. They also have healthy relationships, both with themselves and with others. They are content with their life, and they can find peace and fulfillment in the daily routine.

A day in the life of someone without clarity might look something like this

Wake up feeling groggy and disoriented, struggling to get out of bed. They might not have a clear idea of what they want to accomplish that day or how they want to spend their time.

Start the day with a rushed breakfast and no time for exercise or self-care. They may feel scattered and unfocused as they head to work.

At work, they may struggle to stay focused and productive, as they have a hard time defining clear tasks and priorities. They may have trouble communicating with colleagues and may find themselves overwhelmed by their workload.

During breaks, they may feel anxious and uncertain, unsure of how to manage their time or what steps to take next. They may not be able to relax or enjoy their free time.

After work, they may feel drained and disconnected from loved ones, as they have trouble setting boundaries or communicating their needs. They may also struggle to make decisions that align with their values and goals, leaving them feeling unfulfilled and dissatisfied.

Before going to bed, they may feel anxious and stressed, unable to shake off the feeling of being overwhelmed. They may struggle to fall asleep, and they may wake up feeling tired and unmotivated for the next day.

A person without clarity may feel lost, unmotivated, and disheartened. They may have a hard time setting goals, communicating effectively, and making decisions that align with their values and goals. They may also have trouble forming and maintaining healthy relationships. They may find it hard to find peace and fulfillment in their daily routine and may feel stuck in a cycle of confusion and uncertainty.

Being unclear about one's goals, values, and purpose can lead to confusion, frustration, and stagnation. When we lack clarity, it is easy to become stuck in patterns of thought and behavior that no longer serve us. We may find ourselves on the hamster wheel of life, going through the motions but not feeling fulfilled or satisfied.

Clarity, on the other hand, is the ability to see things clearly and to understand oneself and one's purpose. When we gain clarity, we can align our actions with our values and goals, which leads to a sense of fulfillment and purpose. With clarity, we can make conscious choices that align with our destiny's highest self.

Gaining clarity can be a process of self-discovery and self-reflection. It may involve exploring one's values, beliefs, passions and identifying goals. It may also involve releasing old patterns of thoughts and behaviors that no longer serve us and learning to live in the present moment.

Once we have gained clarity, we can permit ourselves to travel in the direction aligned with our destiny's highest self. This means being true to ourselves and aligning with our values and purpose. It means taking action toward our goals, even if it feels uncomfortable or uncertain. It means being open to the unexpected opportunities and experiences that may come our way.

Being unclear can keep us stuck in patterns of negative thoughts and behaviors that no longer serve us. On the other hand, gaining clarity allows us to align our actions with our values and goals and live in alignment with our destiny's highest self. It's a process of self-discovery and self-reflection, allowing us to make conscious choices that lead to fulfillment and purpose.

Having clarity is genuinely understanding oneself, one's values, beliefs, and purpose. It means clearly understanding what one wants to achieve and what is truly important to them. When we have clarity, we can take control of our lives and guide it in the direction we choose.

With clarity, we can make confident and informed decisions, even in uncertain and difficult circumstances. We can navigate life's challenges with a sense of purpose and direction. We can set clear boundaries, communicate effectively, and make choices that align with our values and goals.

Having clarity also allows us to be more self-aware and self-compassionate. We can better understand our thoughts, feelings, and behaviors and respond in a way that aligns with what we believe. We can treat ourselves with kindness, understanding, and respect and be more resilient in facing adversity.

Clarity is not a one-time achievement but a continuous process of self-discovery, reflection, and growth. It requires being mindful, curious, and open to change. It means taking risks and stepping out of one's comfort zone. It means being open to learning from mistakes and experiences and growing from them.

Having clarity is the feeling of knowing oneself. It gives you the confidence to make decisions and navigate life's challenges with a sense of purpose and direction. It's a continuous process of self-discovery, reflection, and growth. Having clarity is essential for living a fulfilled and authentic life.

Clarity is essential for distinguishing between internal validation and external validation. Internal validation comes from within; it is based on our own beliefs, values, and experiences. External validation, on the other hand, comes from outside sources, such as the opinions of others. Clarity allows us to make decisions based on what is truly important to you and what aligns with your values and beliefs rather than seeking validation from others.

Clarity also allows us to separate opinions and facts. Opinions are subjective, based on emotions and personal perspectives, whereas facts are objective and can be verified. This is important because when we can distinguish between opinions and facts, we can make more informed and rational decisions.

When negative thoughts creep into our minds, clarity allows you to label them as facts or non-beneficial opinions. For example, if you think, "I am not good enough," clarity allows us to see this thought as an opinion rather than a fact.

We can recognize that this thought is based on our own personal beliefs and experiences and may not necessarily reflect reality. On the other hand, if we think, "I failed this test," this thought is a fact, and we can take action to improve and learn from it.

Clarity allows us to make moves based on internal validation rather than external validation. It also allows us to separate opinions and facts.

Clarity is essential for living a fulfilling and authentic life; it allows us to make choices based on what is truly important to us.

Having a clear mental space is essential for diving deep into self-discovery and soul-searching. When we can quiet our minds and focus on the present moment, we can tap into our inner wisdom and gain a deeper understanding of ourselves, our values, and our purpose. allowing us to find purpose and set goals that align with our values and passions.

A cluttered mind can make it difficult to focus, make decisions, and take action toward our goals. Distractions, negative thoughts, and unresolved emotions can create a cluttered mental space. Clear thinking enables us to prioritize what is truly important and to focus on the actions that will bring us closer to achieving our goals.

To achieve a clear mental space, we can practice mindfulness and meditation, journaling, and engage in activities that bring us joy and peace. Mindfulness and meditation are effective tools for quieting the mind and promoting a sense of calm. Journaling is a great way to process and release pent-up emotions and thoughts. If you don't have a journal, go to my website, and order my self- esteem. Engaging in activities that bring joy and peace, such as exercise, reading, or spending time in nature, can also help to clear the mind.

I have found that energy healing in particular Emotion Code and Body, the form of energy healing that I am certified in and use in my practice both personally and professionally is an effective tool for clearing emotional baggage from your life. Emotional baggage which I also refer to as unprocessed emotions. Unprocessed emotions are negative emotions caused by past traumatic, stressful, or difficult events that have settled in the body that can weigh you down and prevent you from living in the present moment and cause mental or physical discomfort. Through energy healing, I have been able to release these negative emotions and tap into a deeper sense of inner peace and well-being.

I also incorporate visualization and guided meditation during my energy-healing sessions.

For you, you can imagine a white or golden light flowing through your body, clearing any negative energy and emotions. Guided meditation allows me to focus on specific areas of my body and release any unprocessed emotions that may be stuck there.

After setting boundaries for myself, I have found that visualization, journaling, self-talk, and energy healing are powerful tools for improving myself and enhancing my clarity.

Visualization is using your imagination to create a mental image of a desired outcome or goal. It allows me to focus on what I want to achieve and create a clear picture of it. I use visualization to create positive affirmations and to imagine myself achieving my goals.

Journaling is an excellent way for me to process my thoughts and emotions. It provides a safe and private space to express myself and reflect on my experiences. I use journaling to track my progress, set intentions, and explore my feelings.

Self-talk is another tool that I use to improve myself. It is the process of talking to oneself. I use self-talk to remind myself of my goals, challenge negative thoughts, and motivate myself. I also use self-talk to reflect on my actions and to practice self-compassion.

Energy healing has helped me take my clarity to another level. It has helped me to release old patterns of thought and behavior that no longer serve me and to tap into a more profound sense of inner peace and well-being. Energy healing helps me to clear blocked energy and promote the flow of life force energy throughout the body.

One of the things that took my clarity to another level is energy healing. Energy healing is a holistic approach that works with the body's subtle energy systems to promote healing and balance. It allowed me to remove trapped emotions from my body which has helped me see things more clearly.

The specific modality of energy healing that I am certified in allows me to clear blocked energy and promote the flow of life-force energy throughout the body. This helps to reduce negative emotions, such as anger, fear, and sadness, that can weigh us down and prevent us from living in the present moment.

I can tap into a more profound sense of inner peace by removing trapped negative emotions. This has helped me be more self-aware, self-compassionate, and resilient in facing adversity. It has also helped me set precise boundaries, communicate more effectively, and make choices that align with my values and goals.

Energy healing has also helped me see things more clearly in my personal and professional life. It has helped me gain a deeper understanding of my thoughts, feelings, and behaviors and to respond in a way that aligns with my values. It has also helped me to be more present in my daily life and to live in the moment.

Yes chickie, removing emotional baggage through energy healing allows you to heal from the underlying causes of the trapped emotions. It helps to release the negative emotions that are holding you back and preventing you from living in the present moment.

Energy healing allows you to get to the root of the problem and address it rather than just treating the symptoms. It helps you to understand the underlying causes of your negative emotions and to release them in a safe and supportive environment.

I gained more clarity with energy healing, and everything began to fall into place. I was able to see things more clearly and make more informed decisions. As a result, I felt more in control of my life and more at peace with myself.

Gaining clarity and moving forward can be hard when you are trapped by negative emotions. But with energy healing, it helps you to release these emotions and to come out from the past, to allow a new self to emerge.

It helps you let go of old beliefs, patterns, and negative thoughts holding you back. Energy healing is a powerful tool that helps you gain clarity and heal from the past, so you can move forward with renewed energy and perspective.

As I delved deeper into energy healing, I found that it helped me to gain even more clarity and to see things from a different perspective. It helped me to regain my sense of balance and to reconnect with the universe.

I felt lost and disconnected when I was not aligned with the universe. I felt like something was missing, and I struggled to find my purpose and direction.

But with energy healing, I could reconnect with my inner wisdom and tap into a more profound sense of inner peace and well-being.

Energy healing was my saving grace. It helped me see into my future and align with my purpose. It was the starting point of my journey and the foundation upon which I built my mission.

That is why I wanted to share my experience with you. I believe energy healing can be a powerful tool for anyone looking to gain clarity, find purpose and direction, and align with the universe. It has been a life-changing experience for me, and I hope it can be for others as well.

When we set boundaries for ourselves, it helps us to reclaim our power and to establish clear limits on what is acceptable and what is not. It helps us understand our needs and communicate them effectively to others. Setting boundaries is essential for maintaining a healthy balance in our personal and professional relationships.

One of the benefits of setting boundaries is that it allows us to gain clarity on our thoughts and feelings. When we set boundaries, we are forced to reflect on our experiences and make conscious choices about how we want to be treated.

This self-reflection can bring insight and understanding about what has happened to us in the past and how we can move forward in a healthier way.

Clarity is essential because it allows us to see things as they are and to make informed decisions. When we set boundaries, we gain clarity on what is important to us and what we are willing to tolerate. This helps us to navigate life's challenges with a sense of purpose and direction. We can set clear boundaries, communicate effectively, and make choices that align with our values and goals.

I understand that starting something new can be scary, difficult, and uncomfortable. And that's ok, it is essential to remember that it is normal to face challenges and obstacles with those emotions. It is important to remember that the effort and hard work will pay off in the end, and the outcome will be worth it.

It is important to remind ourselves that it is okay to struggle and to not let the initial discomfort discourage us from pursuing our goals.

Not having clarity led me to make some of the bad choices that I have made, I regret not recognizing the importance of clarity sooner. I failed to see that it was available and ready to enter my life. I was too focused on my struggles and didn't notice it.

Not having clarity also blocked my view of figuring out my purpose in life.

Not having clarity made me feel like I wasn't aligned with who I was, and it was a lot of cloudiness in my life.

So, the first thing I did to start gaining clarity was envisioning what I wanted my life to look like; it was very detailed, and I took time to really think about what I wanted this new confident woman to look like.

So, I envisioned what she looked like physically, how she would talk, how she dresses, how she carries herself, how her hair looks, her attitude, where she lives, what kind of car she drives, how she deals with things in the world, how she responds and reacts to her environment. Seeing that vision of me gave me a blueprint of what that woman was supposed to be, and then I started working towards the things I envisioned.

By visualizing this specific and detailed version of yourself, you are creating a blueprint of the person you want to become. And once you have that blueprint, it becomes much easier to make decisions and take steps toward achieving your goals.

But it's important to remember that this process is not always easy. You may encounter obstacles and setbacks along the way. But if you keep your vision in mind and stay focused on what you want, you will be able to overcome any challenges that come your way.

As I continued to take steps toward building the woman I envisioned, each step brought me closer to my goal and gave me a greater sense of clarity and purpose. Each decision I made and each action I took brought me one step closer to becoming the confident and successful woman I had envisioned.

The more I followed my blueprint and worked toward my vision, the clearer the path ahead of me became. It was as if each step I took illuminated a new part of the path, making it easier to see where I was going and what I needed to do next. This clarity not only gave me direction but also gave me the confidence to continue moving forward.

I found that each step I took not only helped me to achieve my goals but also helped me to build my self-esteem and confidence. And as I moved forward and achieved more, I felt more and more empowered to take on new challenges and to keep pushing toward my goals.

Step two was acting on what I envisioned that woman to be like.

Let's be clear, in the beginning, I wasn't sure of the vision I had in my head, I wasn't sure because all my confidence wasn't there, and in this new journey I was taking, there was fear, but I didn't allow it to stop me or hold me back I took action and moved forward.

I didn't allow that fear to hold me back. I didn't allow that fear to be why I didn't go after what I wanted and how I wanted it. In the beginning, the confidence wasn't there. Still, each time I took action, it gave me the confidence for the next step, and my confidence started rising, and my fear started shifting away.

Each time I took action, it gave me confidence and less fear, it gave me the ability to see the next step every time I moved; then, I got to the point that whenever I was getting ready to take action, the fear would still creep in, and it felt uncomfortable.

But I wouldn't resist those feelings. Instead, I would embrace every part of the fear and the uncomfortableness. I would say to myself, yes this is scary and uncomfortable. but that's ok, the more uncomfortable I am the more growth I'm going to experience. Chickies, you will never find growth in your comfort zone.

Now, I experience fear only because it is a natural instinct. The key is to know when this instinct is protecting you or holding you back. Having clarity allows you to know the difference.

Starting a healing journey helped me gain clarity. However, energy healing has been a major factor in the increase of clarity that I have gained over the last several years. I gained 200% of my clarity by removing unprocessed emotions from my body,

The third step I took that got me more clarity was that I started living in the present and not in the past again.

There was a point that after I moved into my new home, I continued to live alone for about 12 years; I would date, but I was just so protective of my space. One day my son asked me how I was able to move forward without being angry or resentful.

He noticed that I didn't allow those traumatic experiences to control my life or interfere with how I moved forward. He wanted to know how I was letting it go so easily; I said to him it would make no sense to still live in the past or hold grudges. What would be the point of leaving a miserable situation to continue to live in misery in my mind and heart.

 I put the past behind me; I think it's important to take the lessons from your past and turn it into a tool to help you move forward.

And this is exactly what I teach my clients to do. Whenever we're working through a past traumatic or stressful situation. I ask them what did you learn and what tool did you acquire from the experience? That's what the universe was trying to show you. You need to take that tool, apply to your life now and move forward.

We will need to make our past a school and learn everything we need to learn from it.

Instead of living in the past, you will have to look back to determine what tool you acquired and what lesson you learned from the incident that has happened in the past. If you do this, it will give you the clarity you need to move forward.

Step four: manifestation. I started manifesting everything that I'd been envisioning in my head, partly because I took action. A lot of time, people don't manifest what they want because the universe knows that they are not ready to work for it. All the things you say you want; you must be ready to put in the work.

Taking action is what the universe expects from you.

After years of energy healing, I'm now able to see to a whole different degree of what I envisioned for myself and what the universe wants from me.

Once we are ready to work, the universe will give us exactly what we need. But the universe must first see that we are ready to do the work by taking action.

If you are doubtful, you will manifest doubtful results. If you are limitless, you will manifest limitless results once you take action.

Reread that please. Clarity and consciousness work hand in hand. the type of clarity I'm speaking of here deals with your consciousness,

There are five levels to consciousness

1. Life happens to you
2. Life happens by you
3. Life happens in you
4. Life happens for you
5. Life happens through you

There are things you must do to reach each level.

Level one: Life is happening to you.

There is a good part of your life you live feeling like life is happening to. Being fired from jobs, bad relationships, and aging for me it was two failed marriages and being the hamster wheel. So, I understand how you can feel like the victim during this level of consciousness.

Level two: Life is happening by you.

During this level of consciousness being in a powerless state becomes too unbearable to live with. You begin to evolve and change the victim's mind state and take control of your life. For example, me taking action by getting off the hamster wheel, releasing things that no longer served me and taking control of my life. During this level of consciousness there is a great feeling of personal power. You're motivated to set and achieve goals.

Level three: Life is happening in you.

At this point you begin to realize that your reactions and control hasn't gotten you the peace and joy you were looking for.

You realize that the healing you long for is within. My transformation journey and introduction to energy healing begin at this level.

Level four: Life Happens for.

This is the level when you begin to see that your life was designed just for you. Your journey is your journey. You become aware of how the universe has aligned your path. You place total trust in the universe. Releasing negative unprocessed emotions, beliefs, and thoughts through energy healing quickly led me to this level of consciousness.

Level five: Life happens through you.

This is when you evolve into allowing life to move through you having joy, peace, and creativity that you never imagined. You can relax and just show up. One of the reasons I started energy was to help people release the negative energy that is blocking them from getting to this level of consciousness.

In conclusion, clarity is a vital aspect of understanding and making sense of the world around us. It helps us to see things as they truly are, rather than being clouded by confusion or uncertainty. Clarity allows us to make better decisions, communicate more effectively, and navigate through life with greater ease. It is an ongoing process that requires constant effort and attention. The more we strive for clarity in our thoughts, words, and actions, the better equipped we will be to navigate the complexities of the world and live a fulfilling life.

Part Three

Peace

"Peace is not something you wish for; it's something you make, something you do, something you are, and something you give away."

- Robert Fulghum

What Is Peace

Peace is a state where the mind is free from conflict, tension, and turmoil. It is a feeling of calm and tranquility that allows us to think clearly, make sound decisions, and engage in creative endeavors. Many people find that they are more productive, happier, and healthier when they are at peace.

The importance of peace cannot be overstated. In today's fast-paced and often hectic world, finding moments of peace and quiet can be difficult. However, we must make an effort to create a peaceful space for ourselves, both physically and mentally. This can involve decluttering our living spaces, setting boundaries with others, and practicing mindfulness and meditation.

When we have peace in our lives, we can better handle stress, overcome challenges, and achieve our goals. We are also better equipped to connect with others in meaningful ways and to build strong and lasting relationships.

But what happens when peace is lost? It can be challenging to find a way out when we are in turmoil and conflict. It can feel like we are stuck in a cycle of negative thoughts and emotions and that there is no end.

Creating boundaries and removing toxicity from our lives is crucial to finding peace and clarity. It can be challenging to see the path forward when surrounded by negative influences, or relationships that drain our energy. By setting boundaries and removing these toxic elements, we can create space to think more clearly and make better decisions.

When we can make better decisions, we often find that we start to improve our lives in meaningful ways. This could involve achieving our goals, building stronger relationships, or finding more fulfillment in our work or hobbies. We may feel a sense of purpose and direction as our lives improve.

Living in our purpose is where we often find true peace and contentment. When we do what we were meant to do, we feel a sense of alignment and fulfillment that can be hard to find in other areas of life. By pursuing our passions and working towards our goals, we can tap into our inner strength and resilience and find a sense of inner peace that can sustain us through even the most difficult times.

It's important to remember that it's a process. It may take some time to create boundaries and remove toxicity from our lives, find clarity, improve our lives, and find our purpose. But once we do, we find peace and fulfillment that is all worth the effort.

Levels Of Peace

Here are the levels of peace you will experience after setting boundaries and gaining clarity in your life:

- Physical
- Emotional
- Mental
- Spiritual

Physical peace refers to the peace that comes from having a healthy body and a sense of physical well-being. This includes having enough rest, exercise, and healthy food, and being free from pain and illness.

Emotional peace refers to the peace that comes from having a stable emotional state and being able to manage one's emotions in a healthy way. This includes being able to feel and express emotions without being overwhelmed by them and having positive relationships with others.

Mental peace refers to the peace that comes from having a clear and focused mind. This includes being able to set and achieve goals, make decisions, and solve problems effectively.

Spiritual peace refers to the peace that comes from having a sense of purpose and connection to something greater than oneself. This includes having a sense of inner meaning and fulfillment and feeling connected to something beyond the self.

It's important to note that these levels of personal peace are interconnected and that a lack of peace at one level can negatively impact the others.

Here's a story on how peace came and rescued me.

When I was leaving my second husband, I was also trying to buy a home at that time and there was this three-four-week period where I was at my girlfriend's house. I wasn't sure if I was going to get approved for the house because I'd been trying to get approved for the past three months. I remember being in the car with my son.

My son was a junior in high school at that time; we were running around trying to work things out and also trying to get the paperwork together for the house.

I asked him, " Do you see how hard it is to get your peace of mind back once you give it up or entrust it with the wrong person? Do you see how hard it is to get it back the moment you trust other people with your peace of mind? This is a really good lesson that you should cherish your peace. I told him that he must be selective with who he trusts with his peace of mind. My situation taught him how hard it is to get it back the moment you lose it.

This is a part of my story that has always stuck with me.

Why is peace important after getting clarity?

Indeed, many people are currently experiencing chaos and uncertainty due to various factors, such as the pandemic, economic struggles, and political turmoil. This can make it difficult to find peace and stability. However, it is essential to remember that peace is obtainable, even amidst chaos and uncertainty.

Creating clear boundaries is one effective way to achieve peace in one's life. By setting clear and healthy boundaries with others, we can protect our energy and time and create a safe space for ourselves. This can help us to focus on what is most important and to make better decisions.

Having a peaceful space also allows us to create positivity in our lives and achieve our goals. We can think clearly, problem-solve, and pursue our passions and interests when we are at peace. This can lead to greater fulfillment and satisfaction in our personal and professional lives.

A peaceful environment provides the foundation for creating and achieving whatever one desires.

When the mind is at peace, it is free from distractions and negative thoughts, allowing for a clear focus on what is important. This can lead to increased productivity, creativity, and motivation.

In a peaceful space, one can set clear and achievable goals, make sound decisions, and take action toward those goals.

You can also create a peaceful environment by engaging in activities that bring you joy and make you feel relaxed and fulfilled, such as meditation, reading, listening to music, spending time with loved ones, etc.

A peaceful space can help promote healthy relationships, allowing for open communication and understanding. It also helps in reducing stress and anxiety and promoting overall well-being.

In short, a peaceful environment is a powerful tool for creating the life one desires. It allows for a clear mind, a positive outlook, and the ability to take action toward achieving one's goals. Creating and maintaining a peaceful environment is important to live a fulfilling and meaningful life.

I can remember that moment I was at peace with myself, I could forgive myself for some of the mistakes I made in life. We beat ourselves up about some of our mistakes and the things that have happened to us. We don't forgive ourselves for some of the things that we did and some of the things that have happened to us; we take responsibility for some of the things that have happened in our life in the wrong way; in taking responsibility, you take responsibility in a way that it gives you your power back, not in the way that you are condemning yourself. Once you create peace you can forgive yourself in a way that is empowering.

It is true that self-forgiveness and inner peace are closely linked. When we are able to find peace within ourselves, we are able to let go of the negative feelings and regrets that come with past mistakes. Without inner peace, it can be difficult to forgive ourselves and move on from past experiences.

Many women struggle with this concept. This can lead to feelings of guilt, shame, and self-condemnation, making it difficult to find inner peace.

It is important to understand that taking responsibility for our actions doesn't mean we should condemn ourselves. Instead, it should be viewed as a tool to empower ourselves and make positive changes in our lives

Also, when you have a peaceful space, you can love and accept who you are the way you are, and that was precisely what I did the moment I started getting a level of peace in my life; I was able to love myself for the way I am, and I accept myself just the way I am. I was able to have patience with myself and for myself.

When you have clarity in your life, you can prioritize what is truly important to you and make decisions that align with your values and goals. This sense of direction and purpose can bring peace and fulfillment to your life.

Simplifying your life can also bring a sense of peace. By letting go of unnecessary possessions, obligations, and distractions, you can focus on what truly matters to you and create a sense of simplicity and order. This can lead to calm and tranquility, allowing you to approach daily tasks and challenges with a clear mind and a peaceful demeanor.

Self-love is also an essential component in finding peace in your life. When you value and care for yourself, you can set healthy boundaries and make decisions that align with your needs and values.

Taking control of your life and making conscious decisions are crucial to achieving peace. By having clarity, simplifying your life, and practicing self-love, you will have the tools necessary to confront any challenge and create a peaceful space for yourself and those around you. Remember that peace is the reward for gaining clarity in your life, and it is up to you to take the steps necessary to achieve it.

Additionally, it is important to remember that peace is not just the absence of conflict but also the presence of positive emotions and well-being. By finding peace within yourself, you will be better equipped to handle difficult situations and find solutions that benefit everyone involved. It also allows you to be more present at the moment and enjoy the small things in life rather than constantly feeling stressed or overwhelmed.

It is also important to note that achieving peace is not a one-time event but a continuous process of self-discovery and growth. There will always be challenges and obstacles in life. By consistently practicing the principles of boundaries, clarity, and self-love, you can navigate; them with peace and ease.

Many people struggle with creating boundaries, so when you're creating boundaries, you want to know that there's a payday for it; if you have those thoughts in mind, then the sacrifice will be worth it.

There is a reward for creating boundaries. That reward is peace; There is a sacrifice when creating boundaries and the truth is, it's not easy.

Peace is the litmus test you can use to check if the boundaries you create for yourself are working because if you don't have peace, then the boundary you set is not working.

What will you do when you are not getting the maximum peace you need? you will need to go back and check the boundaries you set, do an assessment to figure out if you are following the boundaries rules and consequences.

Assess your space and ask the following key questions:

Who's in your space? You're the queen of your kingdom, and no one can take that away from you. You need to access the people or things in your space or your kingdom; you need to know if they are adding value to your kingdom or your space. You need to check if you're allowing them to cause you more stress?

Ask yourself what you need to do to change the boundary to get the peace you are looking for. For example, you set a boundary for an unhealthy relationship. In the relationship, someone lied to you, or they have been lying to you. You set the conversation about them lying to you.

They will always have to be a consequence for crossing the boundary, so if you tell the person, you lie again, I will no longer trust you. They eventually lie again to you and don't feel remorse about it. You will have to go back and reassess the consequences you set up for them; for them to lie to you again, it shows that the consequences are not compelling enough.

You have to understand that the consequences are not for you but for the people causing you stress.

Maybe you decided to set a new boundary by dismissing them from your space if they lie to you again. So, if you haven't reached a high level of peace, you will need to go back and readjust the boundaries you have set up so you can experience the level of peace you're looking for. You must also be aware of the level of access you have allocated to the entity or thing causing you stress and blocking your new level of peace.

Now I want you to note something, it's not as if you're shutting everyone out of your life; you are only giving them a certain level of accessibility, which means they can only have access to you in a way that you desire.

Check if you're also sticking by your rules and see if you are sticking to the boundary you are setting.

And if you are guilty of all the above mentioned, you will need to reassess the actual boundary you have set up for yourself. Because if all the metrics are set in place, you will enjoy a new level of peace and comfort, and nothing can stop you.

You will have to understand that you will not start experiencing peace instantly; it's not an automatic process.

 After setting the boundary and you know that you have done everything right and the peace you're expecting is not coming, here is what you need to do?

Rule number one; there is work involved; once you have created the boundary and have gotten clarity, theirs is that continuous process of healing

It doesn't happen overnight, and again, once you get the clarity, you will be able to see which direction you need to go to totally free yourself from all the emotional baggage you have accumulated.

Another thing to note is that some of the processes are instant, especially when removing a toxic person from your life; you should know that process comes with instant peace.

Once you remove them from your kingdom you realize that the toxicity is no longer there. It feels different, and you receive a level of peace when you instantly remove toxic people from your space. The consistent inner peace you strive for will only come from the healing process. Clarity and peace Are like a rebirth; you will start to feel born again, having a new life.

Peace comes with responsibility; it's not free. You need to know that your life is yours. Once you take responsibility, you begin moving into an empowering state that will help you take control over your life.

Once you realize that you control your space, and you get to choose what comes into your space and your kingdom you realize that you are in charge of everything about your life.

Peace, joy, and happiness are some of the highest vibrations you can live in. When you live in a higher vibration, you can block yourself from some of the negativity that comes your way. You are susceptible to negativity and toxicity when you live in lower vibration. When you live in a higher vibration, you energetically protect your surroundings.

boundaries make you understand yourself at a lower frequency. Clarity takes you to the mid-frequency of vibration. The moment you attain peace, you will begin to vibrate at the highest frequency and that's where true joy and happiness come from.

Energy healing is what I use to relieve myself of the negative emotions that opened me to this new level of life. I used energy healing to heal from those things that didn't allow me to create the boundaries.

The first level of peace was me controlling my environment and not allowing toxicity into my territory. The second level of peace was my inner peace with myself. And the third level of peace is the peace I have with others, especially the people that caused me the most pain in my life.

Conclusion

"Boundaries + Clarity = Peace" is a simple yet powerful formula that can significantly enhance the quality of your life. By setting clear boundaries and communicating them effectively, you can reduce stress and increase your well-being. Clarity helps you to understand your own needs and values, as well as the needs and values of others. It enables you to make decisions that align with your goals and aspirations and to engage in healthy, fulfilling relationships.

By learning to honor your own boundaries and respect the boundaries of others, you can create a sense of peace and harmony in all areas of your life.

Whether you're dealing with a difficult co-worker, a challenging family member, or a tricky situation at home or work, the principles outlined in this book can help you navigate through challenges with grace and ease.

Remember, when you have clear boundaries and communicate them effectively, you are taking care of yourself and creating the space for true connection with others.